This book was donated through the courtesy of

Nancy Martin Graham

Embry-Riddle Aeronautical University Library
3700 Willow Creek Road
Prescott, Arizona 86301

GERMAN AIRCRAFT OF WORLD WAR II

WITH COLOUR PHOTOGRAPHS

Christopher Shepherd
Introduced by
Adolf Galland

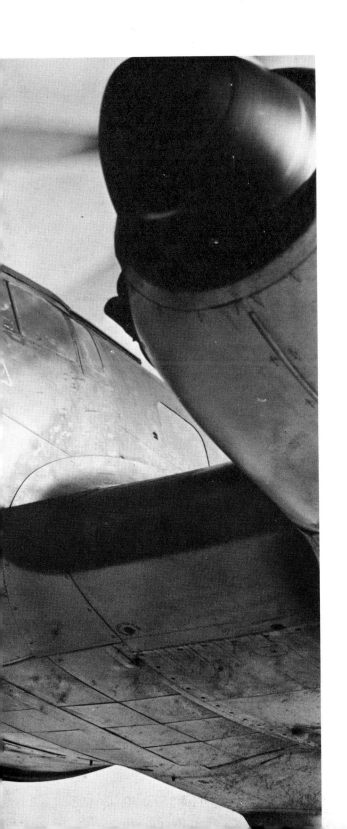

GERMAN AIRCRAFT OF WORLD WAR II
WITH COLOUR PHOTOGRAPHS

Contents

STEIN AND DAY/ Publishers / New York

7/08

First published in the United States of America, 1976

Designed by Paul Watkins
Picture research by Jonathan Moore

Stein and Day/*Publishers*/Scarborough House, Briarcliff
Manor, N.Y. 10510

Library of Congress Cataloguing in Publication Data

Shepherd, Christopher
    German Aircraft of World War 2.
    Includes index.
1. Airplanes, Military—History. 2. World War, 1939–
1945—Aerial operations, German. I. Title:
UG1245. G4S53 358. 4′18′30943 75-26937
ISBN 0-8128-1883-0

Made and printed in Great Britain

Illustrations pages 1-3
Page 1: Heinkel He 113
Previous page: front-gunner lying prone in the nose
of a Heinkel He 111 bomber

Photo acknowledgements
These are arranged in the order of appearance of
pictures. Key to sources is given at end of
acknowledgements.

p. 1 S.V.   p. 2 S.V.   p. 5 Adolf Galland   p. 6 S.V.
p. 8 U.   p. 9 P.T.   p. 11 S.V.   p. 12 S.V.   p. 13
S.V.   p. 14 B.A.   pp. 16–17 S.V.; B.A.   pp. 18–19
P.T.(2); S.V.   p. 20 S.V.; U.   p. 23 U.; S.V.   p. 24
U.   p. 25 B.P.(2)   p. 26 S.V.(2)   p. 28 S.V.; B.A.
p. 29 B.P.   p. 30 S.V.   p. 31 S.V.   p. 32 S.V.   p. 33
B.A.   pp. 34–35 S.V.(2); U.   p. 36 S.V.(2)   pp. 38–
39 S.V.(3); B.A.   p. 40 S.V.(2)   p. 42 U.   p. 43 U.
pp. 44–45 B.A.; B.P.; S.V.   pp. 46–47 S.V.; B.A.
p. 48 S.V.(2)   COLOUR SECTION—selected from
German wartime publications SIGNAL;
BALKENKREUTZ UBER WESTENSAND; and
FLIEGENDE FRONT p. 49 B.C.; pp. 50–51 B.P.;
pp. 52–64 B.C.; p. 65 B.P.; pp. 66–96 B.C.; p. 98
S.V.   p. 100 S.V.   p. 103 S.V.   p. 108 S.V.   p. 113 U.
p. 114 Popperfoto   p. 116 S.V.   p. 120 S.V.   p. 123
Novosti   p. 124 Imperial War Museum, London
p. 131 S.V.   p. 135 S.V.   p. 139 S.V.

**B.A. = Bundesarchiv, Germany; B.C. = Bapty & Co.,
U.K.; B.P. = Blitz Publications, U.K.; P.T. = Patrick
Tilley, U.K.; S.V. = Suddeutscher Verlag, Germany;
U. = Ullstein, Germany**

Introduction by Adolf Galland

Thirty years have now elapsed since the end of the Second World War—the mightiest and most devastating struggle in the history of mankind. Now that the understandable resentments have died down and military historians have begun to concern themselves more objectively and more analytically with the records, the interest of the post-war generation in this whole complex of recent history has been aroused. All the more so as one tries here in Germany to lay the blame for the war as the greatest crime against mankind on the German nation.

It was in fact our former enemies, England, France and America, who first began to write objectively and appreciatively of the colossal achievements of the population and the armed forces. That the Luftwaffe should emerge so spectacularly is due more to their particular role than to their superior achievements. The drama of the long-drawn-out battles, the finally overwhelming numerical superiority of our opponents in the air, led to the inferno which succeeded the chaos.

Many books have been written in the sixties and seventies about the war in the air, the Luftwaffe, their aircraft and the airmen. For the most part the majority of the writers are to be found specifically among our former enemies. Many young people here and abroad have been vitally interested in German aircraft both before and during the Second World War.

Christopher Shepherd here gives us a further illustrated book on this theme, which I can recommend on account of its originality, its superbly reproduced colour photographs and its successful deliberate departure from tradition. I wish the book *German Aircraft of World War II* and its companion volume on *British Aircraft* every success. These two books will undoubtedly be found before long on the bookshelves of many enthusiasts of flying.

REFERENCE SECTION

Arado Ar 196

Ar 196A – 3

Engine	One 900 h.p. B.M.W. 132K radial engine
Span	40 ft 10½ ins
Length	36 ft 1 in.
Height	14 ft 6 ins
Weight empty	6,580 lb
Weight loaded	8,200 lb
Crew number	Two
Maximum speed	193 m.p.h.
Service ceiling	23,000 ft
Normal range	670 miles
Armament	Two 20 mm. MG FF cannons; two 7.9 mm. MG 17 machine guns; 220 lb bomb load

Slightly more than five hundred examples of the highly successful Arado Ar 196 shipboard reconnaissance and coastal patrol float seaplane were delivered to Germany and her Rumanian and Bulgarian allies.

The Ar 196 was designed to be launched from catapults on ships of the Kriegsmarine to act as their protection and long range 'eyes'. When the *Bismarck* roamed into the Atlantic in early 1941 in search of Allied convoys, she launched Ar 196A-4s to drive off R.A.F. flying boats intent on shadowing the German battleship.

The type also operated from coastal ports and it was two Ar 196A-2s of 1./Küstenfliegergruppe 706 flying from Aalborg in Denmark which achieved the dramatic feat of capturing intact a British submarine, H.M.S. *Seal*, in the Kattegat.

Ar 196 units saw widespread service, operating from Norway and Denmark through to the eastern Mediterranean. One staffel, equipped with a mixed force of Ar 196s and He 114 biplanes, flew over the Bay of Biscay against Whitley aircraft of R.A.F. Coastal

Command intent on patrolling the lanes taken by U-boats in and out of deep water. Eventually the R.A.F. was obliged to mount Beaufighter patrols to neutralize the threat posed by the Ar 196s.

The most built model of this versatile sea-goer was the A-3, almost two hundred examples of which were delivered between 1941 and 1943. The B model saw brief service in 1941 at Wilhelmshaven, but work on the C model was terminated before any prototypes flew.

Arado Ar 234

Ar 234B-2

Engines	Two Jumo 109 – 004 b-1 turbojet engines
Span	47 ft 3¼ ins
Length	41 ft 5½ ins
Height	14 ft 1¼ ins
Weight empty	10,802 lb
Weight loaded	22,000 lb
Crew number	One
Maximum speed	457 m.p.h.
Service ceiling	28,873 ft
Normal range	969 miles
Armament	Two 15.1 mm. MG 151 cannons, or two 20 mm. MG 151/20 cannons; 2,204 lb bomb load (normal)

The Arado Ar 234 reconnaissance-bomber was yet another 'last ditch' jet-propelled aircraft type to see Luftwaffe service. Despite the fact it was never delivered in sufficient numbers to be more than an irritant to the Allies, it represented the advanced level of aviation technology achieved by the Germans at a time when the Allies themselves were cautiously only starting to test-fly their own jet types.

Stemming from studies commenced in late 1940, the Ar 234 entered service four years later in the

Previous pages: Dornier Do 215 bomber. Left: Arado Ar 196 seaplanes. Above: the world's most advanced bomber of its time—the Arado Ar 234

reconnaissance role, its first task being to photograph the east coast of England to detect signs of preparation for an invasion of Holland. Photographic sorties over the Allied lines, and Great Britain, had been established on a regular basis by November 1944, the Ar 234 crews having no difficulty in escaping the attentions of Allied fighter pilots thanks to the German machines' greater speed. During Hitler's 'last fling' Ardennes offensive, Ar 234 bombers of II/KG76 undertook pinpoint attacks on various American positions.

A pattern of operations developed in which the Ar 234 was employed to attack the extreme spearheads of Allied advances on the ground, its performance rendering it ideal for this work. It also saw service in northern Italy in the photo-recce role.

Extensive experimentation with the type took place and the sixth prototye was powered by four jets in single nacelles, as opposed to the two powerplants in single nacelles of the service model, the Ar 234B. Further examples flew with two sets of paired jet\engines in preparation for the production of the proposed C series.

One of the most interesting experiments concerning the type was the development of a crescent-shaped wing for the sixteenth prototype. The factory where work was progressing was captured by the British before the wing could be tested but, years later, the design was incorporated by the British firm of Handley Page in their Victor bomber which is in R.A.F. service today in the in-flight refuelling role.

Arado Ar 240/Ar 440

Ar 240C-0

Engines	Two 1,750 h.p. DB 603A-2 engines
Span	54 ft 5½ ins
Length	43 ft 9½ ins
Height	12 ft 11½ ins
Weight empty	18,695 lb
Weight loaded	23,258 lb
Crew number	Two
Maximum speed	454 m.p.h. (with power boost)
Service ceiling	34,450 ft
Normal range	1,162 miles
Armament	Four 20 mm. MG 151 cannons; four 13 mm. MG 131 machine guns

Ar 440A-0

Engines	Two 1,900 h.p. DB 603G engines
Span	53 ft 4½ ins
Length	46 ft 10¼ ins
Height	13 ft 1½ ins
Weight empty	20,282 lb
Weight loaded	26,896 lb
Crew number	Two
Maximum speed	467 m.p.h. (with power boost)
Service ceiling	34,450 ft
Normal range	1,162 miles
Armament	Two 30 mm. MK 108 cannons; two 20 mm. MG 151 cannons

Below: A tri-engined Blohm und Voss Bv 138 flying boat lifting off a turbulent sea

Although few actual examples of the Arado Ar 240 were delivered to Luftwaffe units, the Ar 240 and its companion version, the Ar 440, were probably projected in as many roles as undertaken by any major aircraft type which enjoyed a more successful career.

The roles envisaged for the two machines grew like mushrooms after a shower, and included those of dive-bombing, reconnaissance, heavy fighter, night fighter, light bomber and fighter-bomber. To a certain extent, the Ar 240's weakness lay in its very versatility, the German Air Ministry (the R.L.M.) being unable to decide for which role the type was best suited.

The Ar 240V1 (the first prototype) was intended to include the advanced design feature of a remotely-controlled barbette. In the event this was not included, although the V1 did fly with an interesting 'umbrella'-type dive brake at the extreme rear of its fuselage. The aircraft proved to possess terrible handling characteristics which necessitated much redesign. The Ar 240V3 did include dorsal and ventral barbettes, each containing two machine guns, but lack of stability still showed itself to be present, once again making redesign necessary. The type was then tested in action by a Luftwaffe unit on the Channel. Prototypes for the B series flew in late 1942 and for the C series early the following year. Although the latter series was proposed in a wide variety of roles, work on the Ar 240 was then abandoned in favour of the Ar 440.

The Ar 440V1 was first flown in the summer of 1942,

the type having been developed in parallel with the Ar 240. Despite the Ar 440's enthusiastic reception by its Luftwaffe test-pilot, the R.L.M. decided against further development and the type was dropped.

Blohm und Voss Bv 138

Bv 138C-1

Engines	Three 700 h.p. Jumo 205D inline engines
Span	88 ft 7 ins
Length	72 ft 3 ins
Weight empty	17,820 lb
Weight loaded	34,100 lb
Crew number	Five
Maximum speed	170 m.p.h.
Service ceiling	18,700 ft
Normal range	2,000 miles (maximum)
Armament	Two 20 mm. MG 151 cannons; one 13 mm. MG 131 machine gun; 660 lb bomb load (maximum), or four depth charges, or two sea mines

Nicknamed 'Der Fliegende Holzschuh' (The Fying Clog) by Luftwaffe personnel, the tri-engined Bv 138 long-range flying boat formed an important part of the Luftwaffe's maritime reconnaissance forces.

Below: A Blohm und Voss Bv 138 flying boat, photographed in 1942, undergoing some minor servicing. Right: A Dornier Do 215 photographed in 1940. Below right: A crew member seen through the angular nose panels of a Dornier Do 215

First flying in July 1937, the type was to experience protracted teething troubles which delayed its widespread operational service until the end of 1941. But once the troubles were overcome, it speedily proved a most effective warplane. Allied convoys running war materials to Soviet ports were often first sighted by Bv 138 crews who shadowed the ships and reported their positions to U-boats and German surface vessels. The Royal Navy countered this threat by introducing a force of Sea Hurricane fighters aboard H.M.S. *Avenger* in September 1942, but, although the sightings declined, the Bv 138 was not fully prevented from doing its work. One Bv 138 fought a ninety-minute running battle with a force of Sea Hurricanes but still succeeded in returning to its base.

Much Allied convoy activity was known by Germany to be taking place in the Kara Sea in 1943. Two U-boats were used to establish a base for use by Bv 138s on the little Russian island of Novaya Zemlya in the Arctic, and, a short while later, the Bv 138s began their reconnaissance flights from the base in search of surface vessels.

Thanks to its remarkable ability to stay in the air for a maximum of no less than eighteen hours, the Bv 138 could cover a wide search area in the course of each flight. Rendezvousing with submarines at sea and taking on fuel from them increased the duration of many operational flights.

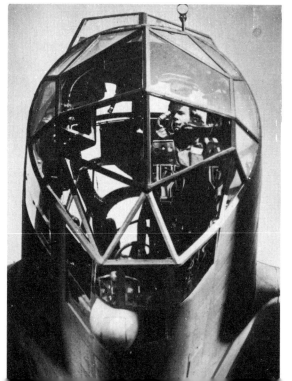

The last area in which the Bv 138 was active was the Black Sea, aircraft of this type still mounting reconnaissance and shipping-protection flights in the late summer of 1944.

Dornier Do 17 Do 215

Do 17Z-2

Engines	Two 1,000 h.p. Bramo 323 P radial engines
Span	59 ft 0¾ in.
Length	52 ft
Height	14 ft 11½ ins
Weight empty	11,484 lb
Weight loaded	19,481 lb
Crew number	Four to five
Maximum speed	265 m.p.h.
Service ceiling	26,400 ft
Normal range	745 miles
Armament	Four to eight 7.9 mm. MG 15 machine guns; 2,200 lb bomb load

Do 215B-1

Engines	Two 1,075 h.p. DB 601 A inline engines
Span	59 ft 0¾ in.
Length	52 ft
Height	14 ft 11½ ins
Weight empty	10,449 lb
Weight loaded	20,282 lb
Crew number	Four
Maximum speed	292 m.p.h.
Service ceiling	31,170 ft
Normal range	965 miles
Armament	Four 7.9 mm. MG 15 machine guns; 2,200 lb bomb load; three cameras

A graceful and beautifully streamlined twin-engined monoplane dubbed the 'Flying Pencil', the Dornier Do 17 started life as a high-speed mail and passenger transport aircraft for use by Deutsche Lufthansa. It proved unsuitable for this purpose due to the slimness of its fuselage, and might have been forgotten but for the enthusiasm of a D.L.H. pilot who recommended that it be developed as a bomber. Thus the Do 17 was rescued

from probable obscurity.

The first production model, the Do 17E-1, entered Luftwaffe service in mid-1937, proving a great success the following year over Spain, as part of Germany's Condor Legion. A new glazed-panel nose was fitted to the Do 17U pathfinder model, the type which later led many night attacks including the one which destroyed Coventry in November 1940. The new nose was retained for the major production model, the Do 17Z, which entered service just before the opening of hostilities.

The aircraft acquitted itself well to the rigours of aerial warfare, although in the face of determined and modern fighter opposition over Great Britain in 1940, it became evident that bombers of all types would lose heavily unless adequate fighter protection was given. This rule also applied to the Do 17.

The aircraft also saw service in the Balkans, against Greece and Crete, and formed part of the Luftwaffe's line-up for 'Operation Barbarossa', Hitler's invasion of the Soviet Union. Germany's Croatian and Finnish allies

Left: Dornier Do 217s being got ready for the next sortie

Dornier Do 217

Do 217M-1

Engines	Two 1,750 h.p. DB 603A engines
Span	62 ft 4 ins
Length	55 ft 9¼ ins
Height	16 ft 3⅔ ins
Weight empty	19,985 lb
Weight loaded	36,817 lb
Crew number	Four
Maximum speed	348 m.p.h.
Service ceiling	36,168 ft (maximum)
	24,000 ft (fully loaded)
Normal range	1,550 miles (maximum)
Armament	One twin 7.9 mm. MG 81Z machine gun; three or four 7.9 mm. MG 81 machine guns; one 20 mm. MG 151 cannon; two 13 mm. MG 131 machine guns; 8,820 lb bomb load (maximum)

A progressive development of the Dornier Do 17 – Do 215 series, the Do 217 entered Luftwaffe service in early 1941, the first new bomber type to do so since the start of the war. A total of 1,730 had been constructed when production ended towards the end of 1943.

From the British point of view, the type is most probably best remembered for the role it played during the famous 'Baedecker' raids of 1942. Bath, Norwich, York, Exeter, Hull and Poole were among the cities attacked by night, sometimes, as in the cases of Bath and Exeter, severe damage being inflicted.

An interesting facet of the Do 217's operational history was the series of attacks it made when armed with the Henschel Hs 293 and Fritz X radio-controlled bombs. The former was powered by a rocket motor but the latter, which saw greater service, attained high subsonic speeds using only the force of gravity. Although a number of British warships were damaged and sunk during Fritz X attacks, the Do 217's greatest success in this field was undoubtedly the sinking of the Italian battleship *Roma*, which was attempting to join the Allies in Malta following Italy's conclusion of a separate peace. The *Roma* jacknifed after her ammunition store blew up.

The Do 217J and Do 217N marks were night-fighters intended to fill a gap in Germany's nocturnal defence which became apparent in 1942. Its long-range, excellent armament and good loiter time proved invaluable in providing the Luftwaffe with another very adequate night-fighter type, even if it was a stop-gap to be employed until sufficient quantities of the Messerschmitt Bf 110 and Junkers Ju 88 became available.

also operated the Do 17Z.

The Do 215 was virtually identical to the Do 17Z, but was intended for export. The Yugoslav and Swedish governments ordered the type but, in the event, these machines were taken over by the Luftwaffe and employed in such roles as reconnaissance-bomber, pure reconnaissance and night-fighter.

Further development of the basic Dornier Do 17 design resulted in the emergence of the Do 217 series of models described on this page.

Below right: A Dornier Do 18 maritime patrol flying boat
undergoing engine tests on dry land. Right: The tubby
yet graceful lines of a Dornier Do 24 flying boat

Dornier Do 18/Do 24

Do 18G

Engine	One 700 h.p. Jumo 205D engine
Span	77 ft 9 ins
Length	63 ft 1 in.
Height	17 ft 9 ins
Weight empt	12,265 lb
Weight loaded	28,000 lb
Crew number	Four to five
Maximum speed	161 m.p.h.
Service ceiling	17,200 ft
Normal range	2,175 miles
Armament	One 20 mm. MG 151 cannon; one 13 mm. MG 131 machine gun; 1,100 lb bomb load (normal)

Do 24T

Engines	Three 1,000 h.p. Brame 323R engines
Span	88 ft 7 ins
Length	72 ft 2 ins
Height	17 ft 10 ins
Weight loaded	29,700 lb
Crew number	Six
Maximum speed	190 m.p.h.
Service ceiling	17,400 ft
Normal range	1,180 miles
Armament	Three 13 mm. MG 131 machine guns; 1,320 lb bomb load (normal)

Probably the most advanced flying boat of its time when its construction started in 1934, the Dornier Do 18 four-seat maritime patrol and reconnaissance aircraft saw rather limited Luftwaffe service, only ninety-nine examples of this type being delivered in the first two years of the war. Due to its poor speed and inadequate armament, production was phased out in mid-1940 in favour of such types as the Do 24. Apart from patrol and reconnaissance, the Do 18 also fulfilled naval co-operation, training and air-sea rescue roles.

Very early in the war, a Dornier Do 18 on patrol succeeded in sending back a message when its crew spotted the aircraft-carrier H.M.S. *Ark Royal* escorted by two battleships and two battlecruisers.

The three-engined Do 24 air-sea rescue and transport flying boat saw wider service than the Do 18 and participated in some major actions. In the German evacuations of the Crimea, Crete and the Dodecanese, Do 24s flew out military personnel and equipment.

In early 1944, Spain bought twelve Do 24s and flew them in the air-sea rescue role from Pollensa, rescuing

pilots of any nationality. After the war the aircraft gradually became unserviceable, but at least one example was known to have been flying as recently as 1970.

Two Do 24s were flown to neutral Sweden during the war, one by a German pilot and his Estonian girlfriend. The other carried thirty-seven refugees to Trelleborg in May 1945. The fate of one of these machines is unknown, but the other was finally scrapped by the Swedes seven years after the end of the war.

16

Right: The night and bad weather interceptor fighter model of the Dornier Do 335 Pfeil (Arrow). Far right: The ninth prototype of the Dornier Do 335—the production prototype for the A-0 and A-1 models

Dornier Do 335 Pfeil

Do 335A-1

Engines	Two 1,900 h.p. DB 603G engines
Span	45 ft 3⅓ ins
Length	45 ft 5¼ ins
Height	16 ft 4¾ ins
Weight empty	16,314 lb
Weight loaded	25,800 lb
Crew number	One
Maximum speed	413 m.p.h.
Service ceiling	37,400 ft
Normal range	1,280 miles
Armament	One 30 mm. MK 103 cannon; two 15 mm. MG 151 cannons; 1,100 lb bomb load

In her battle to stave off aerial defeat, Germany planned many eleventh-hour fighter aircraft towards the end of the war, some of them of most unusual design. One such type was the Dornier Do 335 Pfeil (Arrow) which featured a motor in the nose to pull the aircraft along in the conventional fashion, and a second motor in the extreme rear fuselage to push it.

This arrangement meant the Do 335 benefited from the thrust of two engines while bearing the drag penalty of only one. Its excellent performance reflected this fact and it was, perhaps, a good thing for the British that only small numbers of this potent combat aircraft saw Luftwaffe service.

The first prototype (Do 335V1) fulfilled the most sanguine hopes when it flew in the autumn of 1943. The fourth prototype (V4) served as a test-bed for the projected Do 435 night-fighter, and the V9, which began trials in the summer of 1944, was the production prototype for the A-0 and A-1 models. Test-pilots acclaimed the type's high performance and great range.

The Do 335V10 was the prototype for the Do 335A-6 night- and bad-weather interceptor-fighter model, provision being made for another crew member in a second cockpit behind and above the first. The V13 and V14 single-seaters were prototypes for the Do 335B-1 and B-2 heavy destroyer models. Further models in the B series were projected when the production facilities were occupied by the Allies.

Mass production of the Do 335A-1 and A-6 models were initiated, however, and small numbers were actually delivered to Luftwaffe units before Germany's capitulation, although there is no record of the Do 335's ever having fired its guns in anger. Had the type been available in substantial quantities, there is little doubt it would have presented the Allies with a considerable problem.

Below left: A Fieseler Fi 156 Storch flies down the Unter Den Linden in Berlin in March 1939

Fieseler Fi 156

Fi 156C-1

Engine	One 240 h.p. Argus AS 10 C-3 engine
Span	46 ft 9 ins (unflapped)
	48 ft 4¾ ins (flapped)
Length	32 ft 5¾ ins
Height	10 ft
Weight empty	2,006 lb
Weight loaded	2,070 lb
Crew number	Two
Maximum speed	165 m.p.h.
Service ceiling	17,061 ft
Normal range	205 miles

So excellent were the flying characteristics of the Fieseler Fi 156 Storch, a light multi-purpose communications aircraft, that at times it seemed as if it was capable of breaking the aerodynamic laws governing flight. The Storch was capable of taking off and landing in extremely short distances, it was almost impossible to stall and could fly at very low speeds.

The Fi 156 owed these abilities to its wing's full-span fixed slats and slotted flaps, and a high stalky undercarriage which featured an unusually long oleo stroke. These flying characteristics made the widely-used Storch suited ideally for communication and liaison roles, V.I.P. transport, reconnaissance and casualty evacuation.

Two famous exploits in which the Fi 156 played a prominent part used its flying abilities to their maximum. The first was Hitler's rescue of Mussolini after the Italian dictator had been toppled from power and spirited from hideaway to hideaway by pro-Allied forces. He was eventually located captive in a guarded ski-hotel on top of a 6,500-foot high plateau. After the hotel's capture by parachute troops, Mussolini was bundled into a Fi 156 which had utilised its high-lift low-speed characteristics to enable it to land within the restricted area of the plateau-top. With the combined weight of Mussolini, an S.S. captain and the pilot, it was all the frail Fi 156 could do to take off at all. But it did succeed, and thus Italy became divided in her loyalties, half following Mussolini and half the Allies.

The second exploit saw a Fi 156 flown by a woman, Hanna Reitsch, who landed under Russian artillery shells in the heart of surrounded Berlin to deliver von Greim to Hitler's underground bunker. Von Greim was promoted commander of the Luftwaffe by the Führer and managed to fly out of Berlin again four nights later.

The Storch has been flown by many other countries including Spain, Italy, Sweden, France, Czechoslovakia and Finland.

Although of unorthodox configuration, the Focke-Wulf Fw 189 (left) was popular with its crews, thanks to its strength and manoeuvrability. Bottom: The extensively glazed cockpit of the Focke-Wulf Fw 189 gave its crew unrivalled visibility

Focke-Wulf Fw 189

Fw 189A-1

Engines	Two 450 h.p. Argus As 410-A1 inline engines
Span	60 ft 5 ins
Length	39 ft 4 ins
Weight empty	5,930 lb
Weight loaded	8,700 lb
Crew number	Three
Maximum speed	221 m.p.h.
Service ceiling	27,550 ft
Normal range	430 miles
Armament	Two 7.9 mm. MG 17 machine guns; two 7.9 mm. MG 15 machine guns; 220 lb bomb load

Although Air Ministry officials raised their eyebrows at the Fw 189's unorthodox twin-boom configuration when designer Kurt Tank put forward his proposals for a twin-engined reconnaissance and army co-operation aircraft in 1937, the type proved to be a firm favourite with its crews, thanks to its great versatility, reliability, strength and manoeuvrability.

The aircraft was destined to spend almost all its operational career on the Soviet front, helping pinpoint the whereabouts of Russian units and reporting their positions to the Wermacht. The aircraft's design could not have been better for the reconnaissance role, the crew of three sitting in a veritable 'greenhouse', which afforded excellent visibility half-perched on top of the wing. It was the Fw 189's large glazed cockpit which led to its being dubbed 'Das Fliegende Auge' or 'the Flying Eye'.

A requirement for an aircraft to fulfil the assault or close-support role resulted in an interesting experiment in which the central nacelle of the Fw 189 became a tiny closed-in heavily-armoured box. The pilot was obliged to squint through small armoured glass panels, while the gunner actually fired through a little opening in an armoured visor. As should perhaps have been foreseen, the aircraft's performance suffered heavily as a result of the extra weight of the armour plating incorporated in the central section.

Total production of the Fw 189 amounted to 828 machines, excluding the prototypes. Examples were supplied to Hungary which operated them alongside German units on the Soviet front, and Slovakia.

Focke-Wulf Fw 190/Tank Ta 152

Fw 190A-8

Engine	One 2,100 h.p. B.M.W. 801D-2 engine
Span	34 ft 5½ ins
Length	29 ft 4⅜ ins
Height	13 ft
Weight empty	7,000 lb
Weight loaded	10,800 lb
Crew number	One
Maximum speed	408 m.p.h.
Service ceiling	37,400 ft
Normal range	500 miles
Armament	Four 20 mm. MG 151 cannons; two 13 mm. MG 131 machine guns

Fw 190A-9

Engine	One 2,000 h.p. B.M.W. 801F engine
Span	34 ft 5½ ins
Length	29 ft 4⅜ ins
Height	13 ft
Weight empty	7,180 lb
Weight loaded	10,800 lb
Crew number	One
Maximum speed	416 m.p.h.
Service ceiling	37,400 ft
Normal range	482 miles
Armament	As for Fw 190A-8

Fw 190D-9

Engine	One 2,240 h.p. Jumo 213A-1 engine
Span	34 ft 5½ ins
Length	32 ft 9¾ ins
Height	13 ft
Weight loaded	9,646 lb
Crew number	One
Maximum speed	432 m.p.h.
Service ceiling	37,080 ft
Normal range	642 miles
Armament	Two 20 mm. MG 151 cannons; two 13 mm. MG 131 machine guns; 1,100 lb bomb load (normal)

Fw 190F-2

Engine	One 1,800 h.p. B.M.W. 801D-2 engine
Span	34 ft 5½ ins
Length	29 ft 4⅜ ins
Height	13 ft
Weight loaded	10,800 lb
Crew number	One

Right: Two Focke-Wulf Fw 190 single-seat fighters.
Below right: Focke-Wulf Fw 200 Kondor long-range
maritime reconnaissance-bomber

Maximum speed	410 m.p.h.
Service ceiling	34,700 ft
Armament	As for Fw 190D-9

Tank Ta 152C-1

Engine	One 1,820 h.p. DB 603LA engine
Span	36 ft 1 in.
Length	35 ft 5½ ins
Weight loaded	11,684 lb (normal)
Crew number	One
Maximum speed	463 m.p.h.
Service ceiling	40,300 ft
Normal range	590 miles
Armament	Four 20 mm. MG 151 cannons; one 30 mm. MK 108 cannon; 1,100 lb bomb load (normal)

The second most constructed German wartime fighter aircraft, the Focke-Wulf Fw 190, was perhaps accorded even greater respect by Allied pilots than the aircraft with which it will always be associated in Luftwaffe service, the Messerschmitt Bf 109. Like its cousin, the Fw 190 saw extensive service on all fronts, some 20,000 being constructed between 1941 and the end of the war.

It started life by establishing an immediate and marked superiority over the Spitfire V, a superiority it was to maintain for no less than two years. Faster than both the Spitfire and Bf 109, it soon built for itself the formidable reputation it was to retain throughout the War.

The fighter-bomber and ground-attack aircraft was as important on the Soviet front as the pure fighter. Bomb-carrying Fw 190s flew against the Russians from late 1943, sometimes replacing the highly vulnerable Junkers Ju 87 in these roles. It was superior in quality to opposing Soviet fighters, but faithfully reflected the Luftwaffe's general dilemma in the east, that of being constantly outnumbered.

The Fw 190 also achieved success against B-17 Fortress formations in the west. Due to its generally better performance, it was able to tackle escorting American fighters on somewhat more equal terms than the Messerschmitt Bf 109.

The Fw 190D-9 'Dora' was a long-nosed re-engined model which entered service in the summer of 1944. It must have been irksome in the extreme for Luftwaffe personnel to see their D-9s starved of fuel just when the aircraft was matching any fighter the Allies could produce, including the P-51 Mustang.

The Tank Ta 152 (named after Kurt Tank, designer of the Fw 190) incorporated extensive redesign and re-engining. It proved capable of phenomenal

performance, including a maximum speed of 463 m.p.h. Kurt Tank himself was 'bounced' by three P-51s when testing an example of the Ta 152 late in 1944. By using its water-methanol injection, he left the bewildered American fighters milling around in empty space, so speedily did the Ta 152 show them a clean pair of heels. But, in yet another case of 'too little, too late', only sixty-seven examples of the type were delivered to Luftwaffe fighter units during the closing stages of the conflict.

Focke-Wulf Fw 200 Condor

Fw 200C-3/U4

Engines	Four B.M.W.-Bramo 323R-2 engines
Span	107 ft 9½ ins
Length	76 ft 11½ ins
Height	20 ft 8 ins
Weight loaded	50,045 lb
Crew number	Eight
Maximum speed	224 m.p.h.
Service ceiling	19,000 ft
Normal range	2,210 miles
Armament	Two 7.9 mm. MG 15 machine guns; three 13 mm. MG 131 machine guns; one 20 mm. MG 151 machine gun; 4,620 lb maximum bomb load

The Fw 200 long-range reconnaissance-bomber will long be regarded as the 'Scourge of the Atlantic', the aircraft which hunted down Allied convoys and either bombed them or betrayed their positions to lurking U-boats. Although comparatively few Condors were produced, the aircraft succeeded in building a reputation for itself quite out of proportion to the surprisingly small numbers actually delivered to the Luftwaffe. Winston Churchill described the Fw 200 as 'most formidable', and it required a substantial Allied effort to nullify the threat posed by the type.

The Fw 200 was initially produced as a transport aircraft. It was only after Japan had expressed interest in the type modified as a long-range maritime-reconnaissance machine, that the Luftwaffe realised it could usefully employ the Condor in this role itself.

The Condor's career as a commerce raider got under way in early 1941. It succeeded in wreaking havoc among convoys in the English Channel, especially when working in conjunction with U-boat packs. Tonnage lost to Fw 200 attacks mounted.

Early in 1942, the Fw 200C-4 model was equipped with shipping search radar which increased its efficiency.

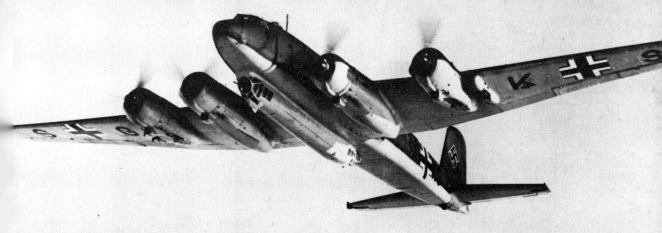

But the Allies were taking appropriate counter-measures, either providing ships with increased anti-aircraft firepower or a Hurricane fighter capable of being catapulted from a short skid mounted just above the deck. Long-range R.A.F. Liberator aircraft were now joined by Mosquitos and Beaufighters in a grand U-boat and Condor hunt. The Fw 200's effectiveness was gradually eroded.

Numbers of Condors were sent to the Russian front in January 1943 to transport supplies to Hitler's surrounded VI Army at Stalingrad. On their return to France, they concentrated solely upon attacking shipping when a definite target had been located, the reconnaissance role being taken over by a Junkers Ju 290-equipped unit. They made their presence felt, although not as keenly as before, especially in regard to Allied convoys travelling to and from Gibraltar.

By mid-1943, the Heinkel He 177 had begun to assume the Condor's maritime role, and by the spring of 1944, the Condors' operations had declined. In June of that year they were recalled to Germany where lack of fuel and poor servicability resulted in very few further missions being undertaken.

Gotha Go 242/Go 244

Go 242A

Engine	None
Span	80 ft 4½ ins
Length	52 ft 2 ins
Height	15 ft 5 ins
Crew number	Two
Armament	Four 7.9 mm. MG 15 machine guns

Go 244

Engines	Two 740 h.p. Gnôme-Rhône 14M engines
Span	80 ft 4½ ins
Length	52 ft 2 ins
Height	15 ft 5 ins
Weight empty	11,244 lb
Weight loaded	17,200 lb
Crew number	Two
Maximum speed	180 m.p.h.
Service ceiling	25,000 ft
Normal range	375 miles
Armament	As for Go 242A

Far left: Hastily applied camouflage adorns a Gotha Go 242 glider. Left: The Gotha Go 244 was, in effect, a Go 242 glider equipped with two low-power engines. It was easily distinguished by its angular box-like fuselage and twin-boom configuration (below left)

in 1942. Although several makes of engine were installed in the Go 244 prototypes, the final choice fell on the French Gnôme-Rhône 14M engine, simply because it was readily available in the desired quantities.

The Go 244, however, possessed some serious shortcomings and only limited quantities saw service in their intended role, being relegated later to the parachute-training role.

Heinkel He 111

He 111P-1

Engines	Two 1,150 h.p. DB 601A engines
Span	74 ft 1½ ins
Length	54 ft 5½ ins
Height	13 ft 9 ins
Weight empty	12,900 lb
Weight loaded	27,400 lb
Crew number	Five
Maximum speed	264 m.p.h.
Service ceiling	24,100 ft
Normal range	1,150 miles
Armament	Three 7.9 mm. MG 15 machine guns

He 111H-6

Engines	Two 1,340 h.p. Jumo 211F-2 engines
Span	74 ft 1½ ins
Length	54 ft 5½ ins
Height	13 ft 9 ins
Weight empty	14,400 lb
Weight loaded	27,400 lb
Crew number	Five
Maximum speed	258 m.p.h.
Service ceiling	25,500 ft
Normal range	1,740 miles
Armament	One 20 mm. MG FF cannon; five 7.9 mm. MG 15 machine guns; one 7.9 mm. MG 17 machine gun

He 111H-20

Engines	Two 1,750 h.p. Jumo 213E-1 engines
Span	74 ft 1½ ins
Length	54 ft 5½ ins
Height	13 ft 9 ins
Weight empty	17,800 lb
Weight loaded	32,270 lb
Crew number	Five
Maximum speed	295 m.p.h.
Service ceiling	32,800 ft
Normal range	1,740 miles
Armament	Three 13 mm. MG 131 machine guns; two 7.9 mm. MG 81 machine guns

Every major combatant in the Second World War appreciated the advantages of possessing large numbers of unpowered, towed, glider aircraft to drop parachutists around strongpoints of enemy resistance, or such features of tactical importance as bridges, airfields, ports or supply dumps.

Thus, German Air Ministry officials pressed for the design and speedy development of a glider with a large hold, capable of dropping parachutists or carrying cargo.

Prototypes first flew in the spring of 1941, and such was the pace of development that no less than 253 examples of the Go 242 glider had been received by the Luftwaffe by the end of that year. The type saw action on the eastern front for the first time early in 1942, when supplies were delivered to surrounded German ground forces in the Kholm pocket. Two years later, the Go 242 once again found itself aiding beleaguered German forces when it supplied food and equipment to the 1st Panzer Army cut off by the Russians at Kamenez-Podolsk. Glider forces were also used by the Germans in the evacuation of the Crimea.

A proposal to 'deglideries' the Go 242 by giving it a pair of medium-power piston engines was approved

Below: Early model Heinkel He 111 bombers with Junkers Ju 52 tri-engined transport aircraft in background. Although affording the crews good visibility, the Heinkel He 111's overall glazed nose (right) often made them feel extremely vulnerable

A most effective medium bomber in Spain and at the
start of the Second World War, the Heinkel He 111
was destined to soldier on long past the point at which
it should have been retired from service. This was due
to the non-appearance of replacement types such as the
Heinkel He 177 and Junkers Ju 288.

Its ability to outrun opposing fighter aircraft in combat
over Spain during the Civil War led Luftwaffe leaders
to imagine this success could later be repeated in other
combat scenarios. Hitler's lightning victories in 1940 did
nothing to dispel this illusion, but during the Battle of
Britain, the He 111 formations speedily showed the theory
to be invalid, as the type proved vulnerable to the
attentions of Spitfires and Hurricanes.

The type saw great success as a torpedo-bomber, and
was widely used with effect against Anglo-American
convoys supplying Russia with war materials. It also saw
service, albeit with less success, in the missile-launching
role, 865 FZG-76 flying bombs being launched against
London by He 111s flying at night over the North Sea.

More advanced types such as another Heinkel design,
the Heinkel He 177 Griffon, never materialised in
sufficient numbers, and although the He 111 was twice
taken off the production lines it was through necessity
reinstated both times. Approaching obsolescence by 1940,
it actually became more or less obsolete two years later.

Mention must be made of the 'Zwilling' twin-He 111.
This was, in effect, two conventional machines stuck
together with an extra engine in the middle (making five
engines in all). It was intended to operate as a glider-tug
and in the bomber, reconnaissance and anti-shipping
roles. In the event, only a dozen 'Zwillings' were built.

Heinkel He 162 Salamander

He 162A-2

Engine	One 1,760 lb s.t. B.M.W. 003 or 004 turbojet engine
Span	23 ft 7¾ ins
Length	29 ft 8½ ins
Weight loaded	5,480 lb (normal)
	5,940 lb (maximum)
Crew number	One
Maximum speed	522 m.p.h.
Service ceiling	39,400 ft
Normal range	410 miles
Armament	Two 20 mm. MG 151/20 cannons

The Heinkel He 162 Salamander or Volksjäger (People's
Fighter) was designed as an easy-to-build simple-to-fly
high-performance jet-fighter aircraft capable of being
produced 'en masse' by semi-skilled labour and flown
by young recruits with minimum training.

It is remarkable in aviation history for the shortness
of its development period, a mere four months elapsing
between the issue of the specification for the type and
the start of production.

The specification, issued on 8 September 1944, called
for a single-engined aircraft with the performance of the
twin-engined Messerschmitt Me 262, able to be speedily
assembled by semi-skilled labour from non-strategic
materials. The German aviation industry was given until
New Year's Day 1945 to prepare for production at the
rate of 1,000 machines per month! Had the Salamander
entered service in large numbers, it would have been

flown by young, and probably politically-indoctrinated
recruits. In view of the urgency of the situation, their
training would have been minimal.

The prototype's first flight took place on 6 December
1944, but disaster struck on 10 December when the
machine crashed during a demonstration before
Luftwaffe and Air Ministry officials. Nevertheless, work
pressed ahead with a slightly modified model, over thirty
of which were built and tested in December 1944, and
January and February 1945.

The first unit to receive the Salamander was a
test-detachment (Eprobungskommando 162) which
joined forces with the Messerschmitt 262- equipped
Jagdverband 44. Jagdgeschwader J.G. 1 also took
deliveries of the He 162, becoming operational on 14
April, 1945. The unit was as good as grounded, however,
by the terrible fuel shortage, and the generally chaotic
state of the Luftwaffe. Leck, the airfield from which the
unit 'operated', was captured by British troops.

Although there is no record of the Salamander's having
fired its guns in anger, the very production of this aircraft
at such a late stage of the War, and under such adverse
conditions, stands as a tribute to German ingenuity and
determination.

Heinkel He 177 Griffon

He 177A-5/R2

Engines	Two 2,750 h.p. DB 610A-1/B-1 engines (A-1 port, B-1 starboard)
Span	103 ft 1¾ ins
Length	66 ft 11⅛ ins
Height	20 ft 11⅞ ins
Weight empty	37,038 lb
Weight loaded	68,343 lb
Crew number	Six
Maximum speed	303 m.p.h.
Service ceiling	26,250 ft
Normal range	3,417 miles (carrying two Hs 293 missiles)
Armament	Two 20 mm. MG 151 cannons; three 13 mm. MG 131 machine guns; three 7.9 mm. MG 81 machine guns; 13,200 lb bomb load (maximum)

Germany's hopes of producing a four-engined strategic
bomber – the Luftwaffe's equivalent of Britain's
Lancaster or America's Fortress – centred around Ernst
Heinkel's He 177 Griffon (Grief).

The Reich's dreams were never to be realised, however.
Dogged by serious technical difficulties throughout its
development and operational life, the He 177 never
obliterated London or Moscow as the Allied four-engined
types did Berlin. Over a thousand examples were to be
built, but it is doubtful if more than two hundred of
them ever saw action.

The brainchild of Heinkel's chief designer, Siegfried
Guenther, the He 177 included a number of unusual
features, including the pairing of four engines into two
couples by means of a clutch arrangement, and an
evaporative engine-cooling method. The latter was soon
dropped, but the unusual engine arrangement was
retained. The coupled-engine system never really worked,
with the result that the type experienced sudden engine
fires throughout its career.

Below: Probably the best piston-engined night fighter
of the War—the Heinkel He 219 Uhu

Right: Although biplanes soon became an anachronism
in the 1939–45 conflict, the Henschel Hs 123 ground
attack aircraft was regarded with affection for its sheer
toughness

The He 177 was ordered into mass production in 1943,
well before its technical difficulties had been resolved,
so pressing was the Luftwaffe's need for a long-range
bomber. After a disastrous mid-winter period of service
on the Russian front, He 177s saw action in the
anti-shipping role, where they scored some hits using
glider bombs, although at heavy cost to themselves. The
Griffon also participated in 'Operation Steinbock',
Hitler's renewed bomber offensive against London in
early 1944, but without great success.

Just before the Russians' summer offensive of 1944,
He 177s struck at enemy supply lines. When the Soviet
offensive swept all before it, the Griffons' aircrews were
ordered to take their big bombers into action as
tank-destroyers, a role for which the aircraft was entirely
unsuited. Large numbers were lost to Soviet fighter
aircraft.

The chronic fuel shortage soon meant existing
quantities had to be reserved for German fighters, the
bombers being recalled to the Fatherland where they
stood idle and unused. The Griffon did not escape this
fate; at the end of the war, German aircraft parks
contained large numbers of the He 177, the aircraft which
was to have been the core of the Luftwaffe's projected
strategic bombing force.

Heinkel He 219 Uhu

He 219A-7/R1

Engines	Two 1,900 h.p. DB 603G engines
Span	60 ft 8$\frac{1}{3}$ ins
Length	50 ft 11$\frac{3}{4}$ ins
Height	13 ft 5$\frac{1}{2}$ ins
Weight empty	24,629 lb
Weight loaded	33,730 lb
Crew number	Two
Maximum speed	416 m.p.h.
Service ceiling	40,000 ft
Normal range	1,243 miles
Armament	Four 30 mm. MK 108 cannons; two 30 mm. MK 103 cannons; two 20 mm. MG 151 cannons

An advanced aircraft possessed of a superlative
performance, the Heinkel He 219 Uhu (Eagle Owl) can
lay claim to having been the best night-fighter of the
Second World War. But for official procrastination and
bickering within the German Air Ministry, it might have
entered service in sufficient numbers to repel the R.A.F.'s
mounting nocturnal bombing raids.

In the event, less than three hundred He 219s were produced, and they therefore never succeeded in replacing earlier night-fighter types such as the Messerschmitt Bf 110.

When, in 1940, Ernst Heinkel designed a fast twin-engined multi-purpose aircraft, Air Ministry chiefs thought the Luftwaffe could win in the War with existing models. A memorandum was circulated recommending the He 219 as a specialised night-fighter, but official interest waned and a further year of growing British night attacks was required before the project was re-examined. A serious setback was sustained when the design drawings were destroyed in a series of R.A.F. raids, but the prototype nevertheless finally flew on 15 November 1942.

The Heinkel He 219 emerged the winner in comparison trials held in January 1943. Generalfeldmarschall Erhard Milch, however, favoured the Junkers design and tried to sabotage the He 219's future. At the critical moment, a major defect appeared in the Junkers type and, despite Milch's protests, the decision was taken to press ahead with the Heinkel fighter. In an increasingly difficult war situation, deliveries were slow and erratic.

In May 1944, Milch finally persuaded the Air Ministry to cancel the type, but, in an atmosphere of order and counter-order, the Ministry reinstated the He 219 the

following month. Production remained extremely sluggish.

Those machines that were produced achieved spectacular results. The He 219 proved capable of bettering Britain's redoubtable Mosquito in nocturnal combat, and an He 219 of Nachtjagdgeschwader N.J.G. 1 once succeeded in downing five British four-engined bombers in a single sortie!

Henschel Hs 123

Hs 123B

Engine	One 960 h.p. B.M.W. 132K engine
Span	34 ft 5 ins
Length	28 ft 2 ins
Height	9 ft
Weight empty	3,312 lb
Weight loaded	4,884 lb
Crew number	One
Maximum speed	226 m.p.h.
Service ceiling	29,500 ft
Normal range	530 miles
Armament	Four 7.9 mm. MG 17 machine guns; 1,100 lb bomb load (normal)

The conventional, sturdy and utterly dependable Henschel Hs 123 dive-bomber and close-support biplane quickly made a reputation for itself through its ability to absorb considerable punishment from ground or air fire and still remain flying. Instances were observed where Hs 123s received direct hits from anti-aircraft fire and yet returned to their bases.

Its very lack of sophistication was sometimes its strength. Under adverse winter conditions on the eastern front, more advanced ground-attack types such as the Messerschmitt Bf 109 and the Henschel Hs 129, found themselves bogged down in the seas of mud which most airfields soon became, but the rugged Hs 123 with its fixed undercarriage managed to continue to operate. Although biplanes had long since been deemed to be 'obsolete', in 1943 a senior German general suggested that the He 123 be reinstated on the production lines, so appreciated by the Wermacht was the close support it gave ground troops. Although this suggestion was turned down, the aircraft nevertheless soldiered on in service until 1944.

To the Hs 123s of II (Schlacht) LG2 went the distinction of carrying out the first close-support mission of the Second World War. The type figured prominently not only in the Polish campaign, but also in the western campaign and later on in the eastern front against Soviet Russia. It flew in the thick of the battle at all times and recorded numerous major successes including the destruction, in co-operation with Wermacht tank forces, of two French divisions and participation in the first

and decisive battle for France when German armour broke through at Sedan.

Psychology entered air warfare when Hs 123 crews discovered that their mounts' engines made an ear-splitting noise at 1,800 revolutions a minute. Polish, Belgian and French troops often broke under the impact of this terrible racket when the aircraft flew low over their heads.

The presence of a biplane in combat units was undoubtedly anachronistic in the latter half of the war, but in the case of the Hs 123 its presence at least represented a successful anachronism.

Henschel Hs 126

Hs 126B

Engine	One 870 h.p. B.M.W. 132Dc engine
Span	47 ft 7 ins
Length	35 ft 7 ins
Height	12 ft 4 ins
Weight empty	4,480 lb
Weight loaded	6,820 lb
Crew number	Two
Maximum speed	221 m.p.h.
Service ceiling	28,000 ft
Normal range	685 miles
Armament	Two 7.9 mm. MG 15 machine guns

The versatile Henschel Hs 126 was primarily intended

to fulfil the roles of tactical reconnaissance and army co-operation. Although possessing pleasant flying characteristics, its inadequate armament and low speed meant it excelled only in theatres where aerial opposition was negligible.

In Spain, for example, it very successfully undertook reconnaissance- and light-bombing duties during the Civil War. In Poland, the Hs 126 served in the tactical-reconnaissance, army-co-operation, artillery-spotting, strafing and light-bombing roles. Lack of resistance in the air and little ground-based anti-aircraft fire enabled Hs 126 units to distinguish themselves at minimal cost.

During the Phoney War, several Hs 126 units flew over the Maginot Line taking photographs for intelligence purposes. But as the French Armée de l'Air became more active, losses increased and, with the Focke-Wulf Fw 189 (the Hs 126's intended successor) just around the corner, production of the Henschel machine ceased in January 1941. The aircraft in service soldiered on, however, even though they were no longer given front-line duties to carry out. Some became glider-tugs, others were flown against Partisan groups operating behind the German lines on the eastern front.

One remarkable episode of the Hs 126's career concerned examples of the type supplied to Greece's Royal Hellenic Air Force by Germany in 1939. In November 1941, a trio of Greek Hs 126s were responsible for dispersing an Italian column four and a half miles in length through constant low-level machine-gunning.

Henschel Hs 129

Hs 129 B-1/R2

Engines	Two 740 h.p. Gnôme-Rhône 14M 04/05 radial engines
Span	46 ft 7 ins
Length	31 ft 11¾ ins
Height	10 ft 8 ins
Weight empty	8,785 lb
Weight loaded	11,266 lb
Crew number	One
Maximum speed	253 m.p.h.
Service ceiling	29,530 ft
Normal range	348 miles
Armament	Two 7.9 mm. MG 17 machine guns; two 20 mm. MG 151/20 cannons; one 30 mm. MK 101 cannon

German troops facing Soviet tank formations often had cause to thank the heavily-armoured Henschel Hs 129 tank-destroyer for relieving the pressure under which they had to fight.

The Hs 129's Gnôme-Rhône engines were extremely vulnerable to dust and sand and, as a result, it never excelled in action in North Africa, but in the Soviet Union the aircraft more than proved its worth.

In July 1943, Hs 129s participated in 'Operation Citadel', Hitler's attempt to cut off Russian forces at Kursk. Flying in relays at low altitude, the Hs 129 units

Below: The standard transport aircraft employed by the Luftwaffe throughout the War was the omnipresent tri-engined Junkers Ju 52. Below right: The ungainly but workmanlike lines of the Junkers Ju 52

succeeded in repulsing the surprise attack of a Russian armoured brigade – an outstanding achievement! German anti-tank aircraft destroyed 1,100 Red tanks and 1,300 vehicles during the Kursk salient fighting.

To punch holes in enemy tanks, different models of Hs 129 were equipped with a variety of heavy-calibre armament, including 30 mm. cannon, a 37 mm. anti-tank gun and even a 75 mm. gun built around a land-based anti-tank weapon. The gun was 20 feet long and fired rounds weighing 26 lb each.

Although Hs 129s appeared over Allied lines on reconnaissance tasks following D-Day, the bulk of the aircraft's service remained on the eastern front. Soviet forces had greatly improved their anti-aircraft and fighter defences by June 1944, and Hs 129 casualties rose accordingly, until one in every five machines committed was being shot down. Soviet fighters performed better at the lower altitudes the Hs 129's role imposed on the machine than at greater heights where other types could escape from them unscathed.

Plans were put in hand to improve the Henschel aircraft's performance in an attempt to increase its efficiency and cut down on the losses being experienced. These proposals, which were never realised, included installing more powerful engines, an ejector seat, different armament combinations and a flame thrower.

Junkers Ju 52

Ju 52/3mg7e

Engines	Three 830 h.p. B.M.W. 132T radial engines
Span	95 ft 10 ins
Length	62 ft
Height	14 ft
Weight empty	14,325 lb
Weight loaded	24,320 lb
Crew number	Four
Maximum speed	189 m.p.h.
Service ceiling	18,000 ft
Normal range	930 mile
Armament	One 13 mm. MG 131 machine gun; two 7.9 mm. MG 15 machine guns

The Junkers Ju 52/3m and the Douglas DC-3 may jointly claim to being history's two most famous transport aircraft. The 'Iron Annie', as the Ju 52 was affectionately called by Luftwaffe personnel, participated in such major actions as the Spanish Civil War, the airborne invasion of Crete, Rommel's desert campaigns and the Battle of Stalingrad. On the completion of production it had served with not less than thirty countries.

A heavy-bomber model of the civil Ju 52 was produced for the Luftwaffe in 1934, numbers of these joining Germany's Condor Legion fighting alongside General Franco's Nationalist forces. They flew some 5,400 sorties and dropped over 6,000 tons of bombs.

But it was in the transport role that the Ju 52 is most remembered. It participated in the invasions of Poland, Scandanavia and western Europe on a large scale and,

in the Norwegian campaign alone, undertook over 3,000 sorties delivering troops, general supplies and aviation fuel. Five hundred Ju 52s took part in the assault on France and the Low Countries, the paratroopers they dropped capturing such vital installations as the key fort of Eben Emeal on the Albert Canal, bridges and airfields.

The two operations most intimately associated with the three-engined Ju 52 are the airborne invasion of Crete (Operation Mercury), and Hitler's abortive attempt to get adequate supplies through to the VI Army surrounded by Soviet troops at Stalingrad.

The first represented an empty victory. Although the island was taken, 4,500 German troops were killed and large numbers of Ju 52s shot down. Stalingrad represented a total failure for, under inhuman winter conditions, the Luftwaffe and its Ju 52 transport force proved utterly incapable of furnishing the cut-off army with sufficient supplies.

Despite plans to replace it, 'Iron Annie' soldiered on until the end. Even the Reich's collapse did not kill her for she went on to be constructed and operated by other countries, including France and Spain.

Junkers Ju 86

Ju 86P

Engines	Two 1,000 h.p. Jumo 207 engines
Span	83 ft 11¾ ins
Length	54 ft
Height	13 ft 4¾ ins
Crew number	Two
Maximum speed	242 m.p.h.
Service ceiling	41,000 ft
Normal range	620 miles (maximum)
Armament	Nil

Despite the fact that at its peak in late-1938 there was a total of 235 Junkers Ju 86s in Luftwaffe service, it spent its life under the shadow of the more successful Heinkel He 111.

Both types were constructed to meet a requirement issued in 1934 for a twin-engined aircraft capable of being either a bomber or a high-speed commercial transport.

Flight-testing revealed that the Ju 86 lacked directional stability and that its two diesel engines malfunctioned when the number of revolutions a minute was varied by the pilot. In Spain, where the type saw combat as a bomber with the Condor Legion, sudden drops in engine power were experienced above 16,500 ft. Although the He 111 was soon considered to be superior in almost all respects, Germany did her best to interest foreign

Left: Junkers Ju 87 dive bombers and their crews
shortly before a mission. Below left: A Junkers Ju 87
takes off with bombs under fuselage and wings

customers in buying the Junkers type, and deliveries of non-diesel-powered Ju 86s were made to Sweden, Portugal, Chile, Hungary and South Africa.

One role the Ju 86 did fulfil with resounding success, however, was that of high-altitude reconnaissance. After extensive modifications, which included the installation of a high-altitude pressure cabin and an increase in the wing span to cope with the thinner air, the Ju 86P succeeded in flying for $2\frac{1}{2}$ hours at 36,000 ft, which rendered it virtually invulnerable to fighter interception when it made its first flights over Great Britain in 1940. Reconnaissance flights at great height were also made over Soviet Russia before the invasion of that country. The R.A.F. countered the Ju 86 threat by specially adapting ordinary Spitfire Vs to the high-altitude role, and by May 1942, several Ju 86Ps had been destroyed by the R.A.F. in the Mediterranean. Gradually the high-flying Ju 86 problem was overcome by the British.

So sudden was the decision to remove the type from production in favour of the He 111, that the German aircraft industry was taken completely by surprise and found itself with several hundred useless components and assemblies on its hands.

Junkers Ju 87

Ju 87B-1

Engine	One 900 h.p. Jumo 211 A-1 engine
Span	45 ft $3\frac{1}{4}$ ins
Length	36 ft 1 in.
Height	13 ft $10\frac{1}{2}$ ins
Weight empty	6,051 lb
Weight loaded	9,336 lb
Crew number	Two
Maximum speed	217 m.p.h.
Service ceiling	26,248 ft
Normal range	342 miles
Armament	Two 7.9 mm. MG 17 machine guns; one 7.9 mm. MG 15 machine gun; 1,540 lb maximum bomb load

Ju 87B-2

Engine	One 1,100 h.p. Jumo 211 Da
Span	45 ft $3\frac{1}{4}$ ins
Length	36 ft 1 in.
Height	13 ft $10\frac{1}{2}$ ins
Weight empty	6,085 lb
Weight loaded	9,370 lb
Crew number	Two
Maximum speed	232 m.p.h.
Normal range	370 miles
Armament	As for Ju 87B-1

The spectacular success enjoyed by the Junkers Ju 87 dive-bomber in the opening campaigns of the Second World War fostered in the minds of the German Air Staff the myth that they at last possessed the supreme aerial weapon. Enemy troops were demoralised by the Ju 87's powerful screaming dive, strongpoints of resistance were crushed from the air, armoured formations were blasted with incredible accuracy, refugees were endlessly harrassed: thus the angular Ju 87 forged for the Luftwaffe the reputation of invincibility in the air.

Known as the 'Stuka', a name derived from 'Sturzkampfflugzeug' (a term applicable to *all* dive-bombers), the Ju 87 was, in fact, an extremely effective tactical ground-support weapon only in areas in which German fighters had established absolute control of the air. Once the type was pitted against modern fighter resistance, as in the Battle of Britain, its slow speed and inadequate armament ensured its rapid decimation.

The Ju 87 naturally, therefore, excelled in scenarios where fighter opposition was either minimal or non-existant. After its débâcle over southern England, it went on to score success in the Balkans, over Crete, and against Allied convoys delivering essential supplies in the Mediterranean and to ports in northern Russia.

The basic lesson learned over England was relearned in the Soviet Union. Creating utter disruption among Russian areas of troop and armour concentration in 1941 and early-1942, the Ju 87 quickly added to its list of successes. But when Soviet fighters began to appear in increasing numbers in mid-1942, the 'Stuka' soon found itself restricted to nocturnal operations. Reconnaissance and anti-tank models fared no better against modern fighters than did the major dive-bomber version.

Production was escalated halfway through the War by the non-appearance of projected replacement types, but it fell rapidly in 1944 with the increasing Allied aerial superiority over Europe. Eventually the 'Stuka' left the assembly lines altogether.

Junkers Ju 88/Ju 188/Ju 388

Ju 88A-4/R

Engines	Two 1,400 h.p. Jumo 211J-1 engines
Span	65 ft $10\frac{1}{2}$ ins
Length	47 ft $1\frac{1}{2}$ ins
Height	15 ft 11 ins
Weight loaded	26,700 lb (normal)
	31,000 lb (maximum)
Crew number	Four
Maximum speed	273 m.p.h.

Service ceiling	27,880 ft
Normal range	1,553 miles
Armament	One 20 mm. MG FF cannon; one 7.9 mm. MG 81 machine gun; one 13 mm. MG 131 machine gun; 1,100 lb bomb load (internal)

Ju 188A

Engines	Two 1,776 h.p. Jumo 213A engines
Span	72 ft 2 ins
Length	49 ft 0½ in.
Height	17 ft 8 ins
Weight empty	21,825 lb
Weight loaded	31,950 lb
Crew number	Four
Maximum speed	323 m.p.h.
Service ceiling	33,000 ft
Normal range	1,500 miles (maximum) with 3,300 lb bomb load
Armament	Two 20 mm. cannons, one 13 mm. machine gun; two 7.9 mm. machine guns

Ju 388J-1

Engines	Two 1,810 h.p. B.M.W. 801TJ radial engines
Span	72 ft 2 ins
Length	49 ft 0½ in.
Weight loaded	30,700 lb (normal) 32,350 lb (maximum)
Maximum speed	363 m.p.h.
Service ceiling	42,600 ft
Armament	Two 20 mm. MG 151 cannons; two 30 mm. MK 103 or MK 108 cannons

Right: Junkers Ju 88 engine maintenance 'in the field'.
Above left: Aircrew board their Junkers Ju 88 bomber, 1942. 15,000 Junkers Ju 88s (above) were constructed, more than all other German bomber types combined. The Junkers Ju 188 (above right) was a progressive development of the '88'

The ubiquitous Junkers Ju 88 started life as a 'schnellbomber', a medium bomber with the speed of a fighter, but it proved so adaptable it was constantly called upon to perform roles other than the one envisaged for it. This is reflected in the fact that more Ju 88s were built than all other German bomber types combined 15,000, of which 9,000 were bombers.

The infinite flexibility of its design not only allowed it to fulfil the roles of bomber, night-fighter, intruder, reconnaissance-fighter, heavy day-fighter, torpedo-bomber, conversion-trainer and anti-tank aircraft, but also enabled it to be further developed into the much-modified Ju 188 bomber and reconnaissance aircraft. Modification of the Ju 188 resulted in the Ju 388 photographic-reconnaissance and 'Störtebeker' night-fighter aircraft. Two prototypes of yet another offshoot of this prolific family, the Ju 488 high-altitude bomber-reconnaissance machine, were destroyed at the end of the War by Allied bombing just before their flight-testing.

The '88 family' passed through a bewildering series of marks, projected marks, roles and operational histories, which cannot be described here in full. The major variants should be borne in mind as the bomber and night-fighter models of the basic Ju 88 type.

The Ju 88 bomber saw extensive service with the Luftwaffe from its operational début in 1939 until the termination of hostilities. Generally speaking, it tended to fare better in combat than other bomber types due to its superior speed. The night-fighter contributed so substantially to the effectiveness of that arm that, together with the Messerschmitt Bf 110, it may be regarded as one of the two mainstays of Germany's Nachtgeschwader units from 1940 until the final collapse of resistance.

The Ju 88 was probably the most readily-adaptable military aircraft to emerge from the Second World War.

About seventy per cent of the Messerschmitt Bf 109 production was of the 'G' model: here (left), Bf 109G-1s. Some considered the performance of the Messerschmitt Bf 109F (below left) to be superior to the later model 'G'

Messerschmitt Bf 109

Bf 109B-2

Engine	One 640 h.p. Jumo 210E/G engine
Span	32 ft 4½ ins
Length	28 ft 6½ ins
Height	11 ft 2 ins
Weight empty	3,483 lb
Weight loaded	4,857 lb
Crew number	One
Maximum speed	279 m.p.h.
Service ceiling	31,200 ft
Armament	Three 7.9 mm. MG 17 machine guns

Bf 109E-3

Engine	One 1,100 h.p. DB 601Aa engine
Span	32 ft 4½ ins
Length	28 ft 8 ins
Height	11 ft 2 ins
Weight empty	4,575 lb
Weight loaded	5,740 lb
Crew number	One
Maximum speed	354 m.p.h
Service ceiling	36,000 ft
Normal range	412 miles
Armament	Two 7.9 mm. MG 17 machine guns; three 20 mm. MG FF cannons

Bf 109F-3

Engine	One 1,300 h.p. DB 601E engine
Span	32 ft 6½ ins
Length	29 ft 8 ins
Height	11 ft 2 ins
Weight empty	4,440 lb
Weight loaded	6,200 lb
Crew number	One
Maximum speed	373 m.p.h.
Service ceiling	39,400 ft
Armament	One 15 mm. MG 151 cannon; two 7.9 mm. MG 17 machine guns

Bf 109G-6

Engine	One 1,450 h.p. DB 605 engine
Span	32 ft 6½ ins
Length	29 ft 8 ins
Height	11 ft 2 ins
Weight empty	5,900 lb
Weight loaded	7,500 lb
Crew number	One
Maximum speed	373 m.p.h.
Service ceiling	41,400 ft
Normal range	350 miles
Armament	Three 20 mm. MG 151 cannons; two 13 mm. MG 131 machine gun

Bf 109K-4

Engine	One 1,450 h.p. DB 605 engine
Span	32 ft 8 ins
Length	29 ft 4 ins
Height	11 ft 2 ins
Weight loaded	7,460 lb
Crew number	One
Maximum speed	451 m.p.h.
Service ceiling	41,000 ft
Normal range	355 miles
Armament	One 20 mm. MK 103 or 108 cannon; two 15 mm. MG 151 cannons

One of history's classic military aircraft, the Messerschmitt Bf 109, meant as much to the Germans as the Spitfire did to the British. Able to claim the distinction of being the most-constructed aircraft ever, some 33,000 'one-o-nines' saw service with Luftwaffe Jagdgruppen on every major European front throughout the War.

The prototype of Willy Messerschmitt's low-wing monoplane fighter won a competition in 1935 against three other types, and it was subsequently chosen by the German Air Ministry for series production as the Luftwaffe's standard single-seat fighter. It entered service in the spring of 1937.

Anxious to test the aircraft under actual combat conditions, Germany included Bf 109s in her Condor Legion which fought alongside General Franco's Nationalists in the Spanish Civil War. The type speedily established ascendancy over opposing Soviet Polikarpov fighters.

The Polish, Norwegian and Danish campaigns added to the Bf 109's laurels. Some 850 Bf 109Es were available to the Luftwaffe for the invasion of the west, and they quickly proved superior to their French opponents.

During the Battle of Britain, the Bf 109E's limited range permitted only a few minutes' combat time over southern England, which proved a serious handicap to German ambitions. The aircraft easily bettered the Hurricane in performance, but finally met its match in the Supermarine Spitfire. An improved version, the Bf 109F, appeared in 1941, and this mark equipped the majority of units lined up for Hitler's attack on Russia.

The last major production model was the Bf 109G, which had replaced almost all previous marks by the end of 1942. The 'Gustav' accounted for over 70 per cent of total Bf 109 production and it saw extensive

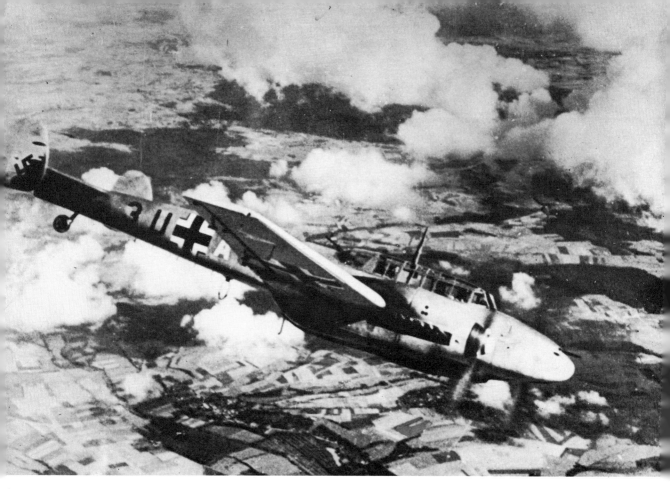

service, especially in Russia and, from the spring of 1943, against American deep-penetration raids against the Reich. The latter represented the Bf 109's greatest test.

With the increasing quantity and quality of U.S.A.F. escort-fighters, the lack of fuel and death of many of their older, more experienced, pilots, the Luftwaffe's Bf 109 units were unable to stave off inevitable defeat.

The fate of the German nation was faithfully reflected in the fate of its premier fighter aircraft.

Messerschmitt Bf 110

Bf 110C-4

Engines	Two 1,100 h.p. DB 601A engines
Span	53 ft 4⅞ ins
Length	39 ft 8½ ins
Height	11 ft 6 ins
Weight loaded	15,300 lb (normal)
Crew number	Two
Maximum speed	349 m.p.h.
Service ceiling	32,000 ft
Normal range	565 miles (on 279 Imp. gal.)
Armament	Four 7.9 mm. MG 17 machine guns; two 20 mm. MG FF cannons; one 7.9 mm. MG 15 machine gun

Bf 110G-4/R3

Engines	Two 1,475 h.p. DB 605B engines
Span	53 ft 4⅞ ins
Length	41 ft 6¼ ins
Height	13 ft 1¼ ins
Weight empty	11,220 lb
Weight loaded	21,800 lb
Crew number	Three
Maximum speed	342 m.p.h.
Service ceiling	26,000 ft
Normal range	1,305 miles (on 675 Imp. gal.)
Armament	Two 30 mm. MK 108 cannons; two 20 mm. MG 151 cannons; two 7.9 mm. MG 81 machine guns

Conceived as a long-range heavy day-fighter, but essentially a failure in that role, the Bf 110 found its niche in history as one of the war's great night-fighters.

Göring's enthusiasm for the zerstörer (destroyer) concept led him to ignore the type's obvious performance shortcomings, which were not dramatically revealed until it met determined resistance in the form of Hurricanes and Spitfires over southern England in 1940. Sluggish manoeuvrability, poor acceleration, inadequate rearward defence and of a size to present an excellent target, the Luftwaffe's Bf 110Cs and Bf 110Ds were massacred by

Far left: A Messerschmitt Bf 110 twin-engined 'destroyer' fighter over England, 1940. Left: The nose armament of the Messerschmitt Bf 110.

Messerschmitt Me 210/Me 410 Hornisse

Me 210A-1

Engines	Two 1,395 h.p. DB 601F engines
Span	53 ft 7¼ ins
Length	36 ft 8½ ins
Height	14 ft 0½ in.
Weight loaded	17,857 lb
Crew number	Two
Maximum speed	385 m.p.h.
Service ceiling	22,965 ft
Normal range	1,491 miles
Armament	Two 20 mm. MG 151/20 cannons; two 13 mm. MG 131 machine guns; two 7.9 mm. MG 17 machine guns

Me 410A-1/U2

Engines	Two 1,750 h.p. DB 603A engines
Span	53 ft 7¼ ins
Length	40 ft 11½ ins
Height	14 ft 0½ in.
Weight empty	13,550 lb
Weight loaded	23,500 lb
Crew number	Two
Maximum speed	388 m.p.h.
Service ceiling	32,800 ft
Normal range	1,450 miles
Armament	Four 20 mm. MG 151/20 cannons; two 13 mm. MG 131 machine guns; two 7.9 mm. MG 17 machine guns

the defending single-engined fighters.

When, however, the Reich turned its attention to establishing a night-fighter force, the Bf 110's adequate performance in the bomber-interceptor role, and its ready availability in numbers, made it a natural choice. By the end of 1940, there were 165 night-fighters in Luftwaffe service, the majority of these Bf 110s. Initially, they co-operated with searchlight batteries, but within a matter of months a chain of radar stations had been built from Denmark to Switzerland. These stations tracked incoming bombers and radioed interception instructions to the waiting Bf 110s. In 1941, radar sets were installed in the Bf 110s themselves, and in June 1942 an improved night-fighter model, the Bf 110G-4, entered service.

To counter R.A.F. radar jamming devices, the Bf 110s tried to infiltrate the bomber streams visually on their way to, and over, the target. A pattern emerged in which temporary advantage was gained by the side with the latest radar, or radar-jamming, equipment.

The Bf 110s maintained their overall effectiveness, however, and on the night of 30 March 1944, German night-fighters destroyed 94 out of a total of 795 R.A.F. bombers attacking Nuremberg.

The Bf 110 gave first-class service in its nocturnal role until the final collapse. If it lost heavily in day combat, it may be said to have evened the score when the moon had risen.

Born of the same enthusiasm for the heavy long-range zerstörer (destroyer) concept which resulted in the Messerschmitt Bf 110, its intended successor, the Me 210, distinguished itself solely by its failure to be of any use to the Luftwaffe whatsoever.

First flying on 2 September 1939 – one day before Great Britain's declaration of war – the Me 210 quickly proved to lack longitudinal stability, a fault which persisted throughout its brief career and which was the major reason for ceasing production after the delivery of a mere two hundred machines.

By giving the Me 210 longer engine cowlings and incorporating many minor improvements, Messerschmitt created the Me 410 Hornisse. The modifications so greatly improved the Me 410's flying characteristics, however, that the type must be regarded in an entirely different light from that of its predecessor. It entered service in April and May, 1943, in the bomber, reconnaissance and heavy-fighter roles, and it established itself as moderately successful in all of them.

In the pure bomber-destroyer role, Me 410s were equipped with an exotic mixture of armament, including a 50 mm. cannon based on that carried by a type of armoured car, a variety of different calibre rockets and various machine gun and cannon combinations. One leading bomber-destroyer pilot, Lieutenant Rudi Dassow, even had his Me 410 equipped with eight 20 mm. cannons!

Such armament naturally proved effective against American bomber formations, and, in a tremendous battle over Budapest, German fighters claimed thirty-four four-engined bombers destroyed, eight of them falling to Me 410s without loss to themselves. But the type did prove vulnerable to the attentions of American single-seat escort fighters such as the P-47 Thunderbolt and P-51 Mustang. On one occasion twelve Me 410s were written off in a single engagement by twenty P-51s escorting Fortress bombers to their aircraft factory target in May 1944.

Intended as a replacement for the Messerschmitt Bf 110, the Me 210 (left) was a complete failure and speedily gave way to the Me 410. The Messerschmitt Me 410 (bottom) was a moderately successful fighter. Below: The fantastic Messerschmitt Me 163 Komet rocket-propelled fighter

Messerschmitt Me 163 Komet

Engine	One Walter HWK 109-509A-2 rocket motor
Span	30 ft 7 ins
Length	18 ft 8 ins
Height	9 ft
Weight empty	4,200 lb
Weight loaded	9,500 lb
Crew number	One
Maximum speed	596 m.p.h.
Service ceiling	39,500 ft
Armament	Two 30 mm. MK 108 cannons

The Komet was the first (and only) rocket-powered fighter to enter regular service with an air arm, and represented the Luftwaffe's greatest attempt to solve by technical means the problem of the Allies' numerical superiority in the air. Its phenomenal performance, which included the then unheard of speed of 596 m.p.h., lent this diminutive warplane immunity from interception from Allied piston-engined fighters.

The safety enjoyed by its pilots on this account was

45

more than counterbalanced, however, by the unpredictable nature of the rocket engine's fuels. These comprised hydrogen peroxide and water, and hydrazine hydrate and methyl alcohol. When the fuels came into contact there was an immediate and violent explosion which, when successfully directed out through the rear pipe as intended, gave the Me 163 its fantastic acceleration, but when unsuccessfully directed, usually blew the machine and its occupant to pieces or merely 'dissolved' the pilot alive!

The Me 163 entered service in March 1944 with Jagdgeschwader JG 400, the only unit which ever received the type. It commenced operations in August of that year and was destined to fight as a unit until March 1945. It was debateable whether the Komets did not inflict more casualties and deaths on their own pilots and groundcrew during this period than on the aircrew of Allied fighters and bombers. When the Me 163 did strike successfully, however, it did so in dramatic fashion. The commander of the second gruppe of JG 400, Major Robert Olejnik, once destroyed three B-17 Fortress bombers in rapid succession over Altenburg in Thuringia.

Allied records show that the type was known to have attacked with R4M rockets, and that one B-17 was destroyed by ten 50 mm. shells discharged from two five-barrelled guns mounted vertically in the Komet's wingroots. Their firing was triggered off by the action of light-sensitive cells.

In March 1945, the fuel shortage caught up with JG 400 and the unit was disbanded. The Me 163 contributed almost nothing to the Luftwaffe's declining effectiveness but it did succeed in establishing itself firmly in the annals of aeronautical history.

Messerschmitt Me 262

Me 262A-1a

Engines	Two 1,980 lb s.t. Jumo 109-004 B-1 turbojets
Span	40 ft 11½ ins
Length	34 ft 9½ ins
Height	12 ft 7 ins
Weight empty	9,741 lb
Weight loaded	14,101 lb
Crew number	One
Maximum speed	542 m.p.h.
Service ceiling	36,091 ft
Normal range	652 miles
Armament	Four 30 mm. Rheinmetall-Borsig MK 108 cannons

The world's first operational jet fighter, the Me 262, might well have turned the tide of Allied aerial supremacy had Adolf Hitler's 'intuition' allowed it to do so. At least 100 m.p.h. faster than opposing piston-engined types, the Me 262 could penetrate American fighter screens with ease and destroy the B-17 Fortress bomber formations they protected. But Hitler fatally delayed its operational début by ordering it to be mass-produced as a bomber!

Undoubtedly, the best-known unit to have operated the Me 262 was Jagdverband 44, led initially by Gen. Lt. Adolf Galland. The unit flew from a variety of airfields within the shrinking Reich, sometimes taking off from autobahns, and dispersing, on landing, to camouflaged forest hideaways. The R4M rockets they carried broke up formations of American bombers with great effectiveness. In order to catch the elusive jets, the

Left: The world's first jet fighter to see operational service, the Messerschmitt Me 262. Below: The bulbous nose of the gigantic Messerschmitt Me 321 transport glider

R.A.F. was obliged to mount standing patrols of fighters over the bases from which they were known to fly, since it was only when the jets slowed down to land that the conventional piston-engined aircraft could catch them. Strong flak defences were soon installed by the Germans around these bases and the whole procedure, from the R.A.F.'s point of view, became one which tested even the strongest of nerves. British fighter pilots dubbed this technique 'rat catching'.

While the single-seat day-fighter model made itself known to the Americans' bomber units and their escort-fighters, a two-seat night-fighter model helped defend Berlin against the nocturnal attacks of British bombers. A reconnaissance version slipped over front lines with virtual impunity to photograph the latest Allied positions. Although the bomber version could usually escape from Allied fighter aircraft and deliver its bomb load, the actual destructive power of that bomb load was negligible.

Messerschmitt Me 321/Me 323

Me 323E

Engines	Six 990 h.p. Gnôme-Rhône 14N radial engines
Span	181 ft
Length	93 ft 4 ins
Weight empty	61,700 lb
Weight loaded	96,000 lb
Crew number	Five to seven
Maximum speed	136 m.p.h.
Normal range	685 miles
Armament	Five 13 mm. MG 131 machine guns

The prototype of the enormous Messerschmitt Me 321 glider was the second largest aircraft in the world when it started flight-testing in February 1941, almost precisely fourteen weeks after Messerschmitt received the green light to proceed with construction.

The Me 321 was specifically conceived to take part in the invasion of Great Britain, and it had to be capable of transporting such items as a PzKW IV tank, a self-propelled gun or an 88 mm. anti-aircraft gun. The firm was given just two weeks in which to produce an outline design, and it was then instructed to obtain all the material necessary for the building of the first hundred examples.

It required no fewer than three Messerschmitt Bf 110C twin-engined fighter aircraft to tow the Me 321 off the ground, a technique which called for considerable nerve, as there was ample opportunity for accidents. One accident resulted in a total of 129 lives being lost when take-off rockets attached under one of the glider's wings failed to ignite.

Largely in order to resolve the problem of getting the Me 321 off the ground, six engines were installed in a powered version, the Me 323, which saw operational service in the Mediterranean and on the eastern front.

Me 323-equipped transport units flew between Europe and north Africa unmolested by Allied fighters, until early in 1943 when one such unit was decimated by R.A.F. fighters, fourteen of its sixteen Me 323s being destroyed. In Russia, inadequate numbers of Me 323s were ranged along vast lengths of the front line. It was intended to use the glider version, the Me 321, in the supply of material to the surrounded VI Army at Stalingrad but, in the event, the aircraft arrived too late.

Below: Loading field artillery into a six-engined
Messerschmitt Me 323 aircraft. Bottom: The
Messerschmitt Me 323 was perhaps experiencing
difficulties with its extreme starboard engine which is
feathered

COLOUR SECTION

The Balkans; a Dornier bomber heads inland

Dornier Do 217 bombers
Overleaf: Crew's eye view; Dorniers in formation

Two of a breed. Dornier twin-engined bombers

A Focke-Wulf Fw 189 army co-operation and reconnaissance
aircraft on the Finnish front

**Left: Crew walk to their Focke-Wulf Fw 200
Condor maritime reconnaissance aircraft
Above: Fw 200 Condor in close up**

Heinkel He 111;
aircrew and nose gunner

**Refuelling a Heinkel He 111
night bomber
Below: 'Bombing up' a Heinkel
He 111**

**Heinkel He 111 nose
gunner's view
Below: Luftwaffe
groundcrew arming a
Heinkel He 111**

Left : The scourge of Europe for the first half of the war –
Heinkel He 111 bombers in formation
An upper fuselage gunner of a Heinkel He 177

A Henschel Hs 126 army co-operation
aircraft over Greece

The omnipresent Ju 52 transport aircraft

**Overleaf: The Junkers Ju 86 excelled
in the high-flying reconnaissance role
Inset: The mainstay of the Luftwaffe's
transport force, the Junkers Ju 52**

Vulnerable when exposed to
fighter oppostion; the Junkers
Ju 87, the 'Stuka'
Below: 'Bombing up' Ju 87s
early in the War
Right: Ju 87s in the Balkans

**Below: A Luftwaffe armourer in typical black overalls.
Behind, a Ju 87 dive-bomber
Right: Late-mark Ju 87s in formation**

The versatile Junkers Ju 88, here in Sicily

Ju 88 in the desert

Ju 88 'revving up' for take-off. Note the bombload

Left: Messerschmitt Bf 109 fighters of JG27 'Afrika'.
Above: How effective camouflage can be; a
Messerschmitt Bf 109 in North Africa

Left: Painting victory tallies
on the tail of a Bf 109 on
the Eastern front
Right: The Focke-Wulf Fw
190; undoubtedly the
Luftwaffe's best single-seat
fighter of the war
Below: Sighting the guns of
a Messerschmitt Bf 109 in
the western desert

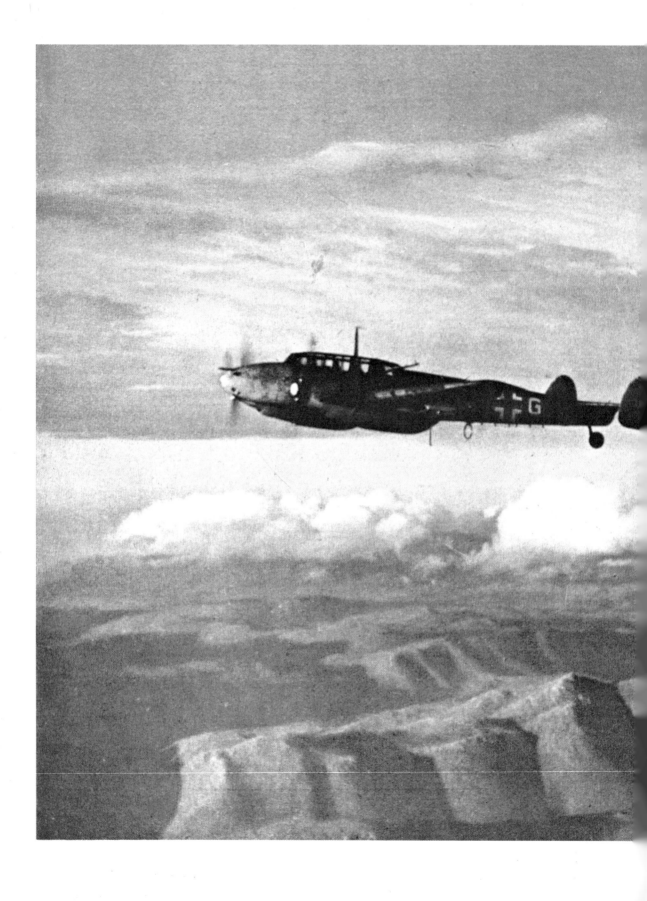

The Luftwaffe over Sicily. A twin-engined
Messerschmitt Bf 110 fighter

Left: Messerschmitt Bf 110 long-range fighters were extensively used in the Mediterranean theatre
Below: More Bf 'one-one-ohs'; this time over France

Bf 110 swirling up the desert dust

**About to load a camera into a reconnaissance model
of the Bf 110
Right: A Bf 110 on a rough Balkan airstrip**

**Messerschmitt Bf 110. Note the extra fuel tanks
under fuselage and starboard wing
Left: Groundcrew load shells into the nose
armament of a Bf 110**

A mix of tri-engined Ju 52 transports and twin-engined Messerschmitt Bf 110 fighters in Cyrenaica

IN ACTION

The Luftwaffe during the
Second World War

A Panorama

When the morning of 7 May 1945 dawned, the cities of the Third Reich lay in smoking piles of brick and dust. People threaded their way like insects through this lunar landscape trying to knit the fabric of their lives back into some sort of recognizable pattern. The cities would be rebuilt, but not the dreams of the Reich. They were to rest buried for ever along with the bodies of many thousands of innocent civilians in the chaotic rubble that was Germany after six years' war.

Could the Luftwaffe be blamed for failing to protect the Reich's towns? Why was Berlin obliterated when London, by comparison, was barely scratched? Why had the Luftwaffe succeeded brilliantly against France, but not against Great Britain? Why had it not been able to prevent the VI Army's fate at Stalingrad, the turning point of the War? Why had German fighter pilots not decimated American bomber formations over the Fatherland? Perhaps greatest of all, why did the Luftwaffe not throw the great Anglo-American invasion of 1944 back into the sea? Why? Why, in short, did the Luftwaffe make European history in 1940 and 1941 and then, in the following years, fail to sustain the changes it had itself wrought?

The answers are many, and some very complicated. But two basic ones are, firstly, that the Reich's political leaders envisaged a short war requiring a tactical rather than a strategic air force and, secondly, that as Germany acquired more and more enemies, the Luftwaffe found itself more and more swamped in the air by numerically superior foes. These are political as well as military reasons.

As a well-equipped tactical air force, the Luftwaffe succeeded against the French Armée de l'Air and ejected the Royal Air Force from European skies in 1940. As the same well-equipped tactical air force, it failed against the U.S.S.R. because only a strategic air force which included a strategic bombing force could have overcome the problems presented by the vastness of the country and its inhabitants' ability to move their industries eastwards out of the range of tactical bombers. Tactical air forces produce aircraft like the short-range Junkers Ju 87 Stuka and the medium-range Ju 88 and Heinkel He 111. They do not have aircraft such as the long-range Avro Lancaster and Boeing B-17 Fortress which, between them, were largely responsible for the destruction of German industrial and civilian centres of concentration.

However, one elementary fact should never be forgotten. Germany faced alone (unless a handful of tiny allies and an impotent Italy could be described as true 'allies') two of the world's greatest countries, the United States of America and Soviet Russia. And as the months drifted past, the rolling plains of the Soviet Union swallowed more and more hundreds of valuable aircraft and aircrew, just as they did tanks and infantry. The finite resources of the Reich were stretched to their utmost in attempting to combat the Soviet forces, who seemed more numerous each day, notwithstanding the large numbers contained in German P.O.W. camps. Small wonder Germany could not spare sufficient aircraft and fliers to overwhelm the growing U.S.A.A.F. bomber threat over occupied Europe. The Italian front provided another headache. How could the Luftwaffe provide ground troops with adequate air cover and protect cities full of civilians on all fronts all the time in really meaningful numbers? After D-Day the situation became desperate or laughable, depending on how you looked at it. The Luftwaffe's contribution to attempting to repel the invasion was totally futile.

Only sometimes can a specific reason, or reasons, be found for the Luftwaffe's failure to bring a campaign to a successful conclusion. During the so-called Battle of Britain, for example, there were two fundamental reasons. The first lay in the decision to cease attacking R.A.F. airfields and start bombing the capital instead; the second lay in the inadequate range of the Messerschmitt Bf 109 fighter, which did not allow single-seat fighter pilots sufficient (in modern parlance) 'loiter time' over target. This denied them the chance to enter sustained combat with R.A.F. fighters.

In the face of facts such as these, one can only wonder at the marvels the Luftwaffe did succeed in achieving. With the help of its air arm, Germany beat her old foe, France, within six weeks; came perilously close to winning the Battle of Britain, which would have resulted in the invasion of Britain; mutilated the Russian air force and swept to Moscow with the Soviet armies in retreat before it; forced the Americans at one point to discontinue their daylight bombing raids through heavy losses; and, at the end, obliged the Allies to put up an effort in the air totally out of proportion to the threat the Luftwaffe could present. Although insignificant to the outcome of the war, it is interesting for aviation enthusiasts to note that the world's first jet fighter unit, equipped with Messerschmitt Me 262s, was formed by the Luftwaffe in 1944.

Many of the inadequacies and shortcomings of the Luftwaffe would have been inherent in any tactical air force forced to perform a job for which it was not intended. What is quite certain is that, as Goering claimed, none were due to the quality of the aircrew themselves. Fighter, bomber, transport, reconnaissance and all other categories of aircrew threw themselves into their appointed tasks with outstanding élan and dedication. Although towards the end it was increasingly realised that defeat was inevitable, they continued by day and night to defend the shrinking boundaries of their homeland with uniformly unfailing bravery.

Crosses in the earth of almost every European nation stand as mute but eloquent testimony to their preparedness to die for their country and for its defence.

Blitzkrieg: the Lightning War

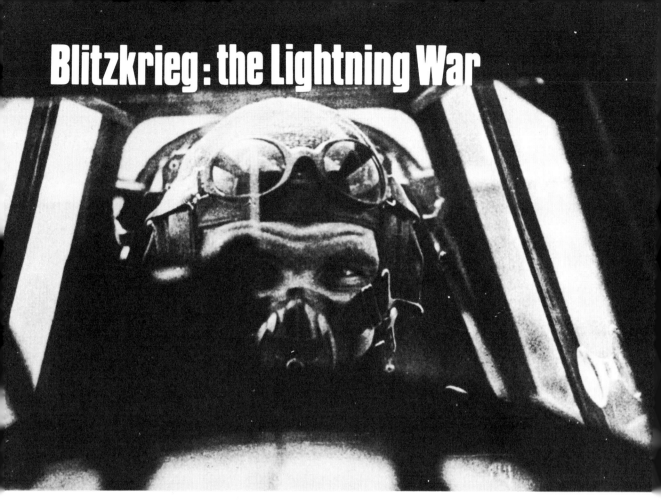

Signed on 28 June 1919 in the Hall of Mirrors at the Château de Versailles near Paris, the Treaty of Versailles had been drawn up by the victorious Allies to include a clause ordering the dissolution of the German air force and the destruction of its equipment. But while Germany staggered under the shadow of massive reparation payments and the surrender of much of her territory, those who had been involved in flying in the Great War were reluctant to witness the wholesale destruction of her air force without the hope of ever building a new and better one.

In 1921 two events of note occurred. The first was that Adolf Hitler took control of the National-Sozialistische Deutsche Arbeiter Partei (N.S.D.A.P.) and met Hermann Goering, a decorated former leader of the Richthofen Jagdgeschwader ('J.G.' or fighter unit) to whom he offered membership of the party. The second was that General von Seeckt, Commander-in-Chief of the Reichswehr, established a secret flying department in his defence ministry and concluded an agreement with Soviet Russia whereby the latter placed at German disposal an airfield with ancillary equipment at Lipetsk, some 200 miles south-east of Moscow.

With the lifting by the Allies on 3 May 1922 of the ban of the construction of civil aircraft, designers went back to work, and within a short time a number of constructors, including Dornier, Heinkel, Junkers, Arado and Messerschmitt, were producing new aircraft types. Four years later, in 1926, appeared Deutsche Lufthansa, Germany's new and official state airline. The manufacturers started producing speedy new aircraft, ostensibly for use by the airline, but, in reality, military types in civil guise. And here the position rested for some time until Hitler led the National Socialists to victory at the polls on 5 March 1933 and assumed the chancellorship of Germany.

The Fuehrer looked to Goering for the fastest possible creation of a new air force, which was to be called the Luftwaffe. Although the existence of the Luftwaffe was not to be revealed to the world until March 1935, Goering flung himself into the job with enthusiasm and rapidly surrounded himself with men of varying ability, such as Erhard Milch, Lieutenant-General Wever, General Stumpff and Karl Bodenschatz. The airfield at Lipetsk was closed, and German aircrew were sent to train under realistic combat conditions in Italy with Mussolini's Regia Aeronautica. New types were selected for production and plans laid for even faster fighters and bombers.

Yet even as events were proceeding so satisfactorily, the seeds of faulty planning had been sown. With the death of General Wever in 1936, the most strident protagonist of the strategic four-engined bomber had fallen silent. And though four-engined bombers were to emerge over the years, no long-range strategic bombing force was ever built.

All that was now needed for the planners to wed themselves to the concept of a tactical air force for Germany was for someone to discover the single-engined short-range dive-bomber. That person was Ernst Udet, a carefree fighter pilot cum aerobatics expert, who came across the prototype of such an aircraft during a visit, made at Goering's suggestion, to the United States. This proved the genesis of the famous Junkers Ju 87.

Fighting over Spain

When the Spanish Civil War broke out in July 1936, Germany seized the opportunity it offered to test her new machines, personnel and theories in practice. Under conditions of utmost secrecy, Hitler sent aid, in the form of aircrew, mechanics, fighters, bombers, transport and reconnaissance aircraft, to the anti-Government insurgent forces under the leadership of General Francisco Franco Bahamonde. Officially titled the Luftwaffe Volunteer Corps, the air element was better known as the Legion Kondor, and, together with aircraft sent by Mussolini, they faced opposition in the form of equipment sent by France and the Soviet Union.

It was in Spain that many valuable lessons were learned. Loose formation techniques, the value of pinpoint dive-bombing, and the effects of 'carpet bombing' were noted, absorbed and used

in northern Europe later on. Undoubtedly, the act for which the Luftwaffe is most remembered was the destruction of the Spanish town of Guernica on 26 April 1937. Saturation or carpet bombing was very much an unknown quantity in those days, and it was to assess the results of such an attack that formations of Heinkel He 111 bombers rained high-explosive and incendiary bombs down on the little city in three great waves. Some 1,600 people were killed, a large part of the town was utterly shattered, and at least one hospital was blown to pieces and its inhabitants burned alive. In fact, the attack was such a 'success' that it earned Germany the condemnation of the world when Press correspondents turned in their newspaper stories.

The Luftwaffe's new aircraft types were tested too. The Messerschmitt Bf 109 single-seater fighter, the Junkers Ju 87 dive-bomber, the Junkers Ju 52 transport-bomber, the Heinkel He 111 and Dornier Do 17 bombers – all were put through the most rigorous test of all, actual combat experience, in Spain with the Legion Kondor.

Turning east

Now the time had come for the Luftwaffe to fight for Germany. Hitler's eyes had always been drawn east towards Poland – the natural area for German expansion – and towards the corn, oil and mineral deposits of the Soviet Union. Moreover, a blitzkrieg (lightning war) against Poland would seal the east against possible intervention by Soviet forces when the Reich later turned its attention to the western democracies and, by necessity, had its back turned.

Blitzkrieg was the theory of warfare that won Hitler his vast territorial gains. It beat Poland and France, and later it was used with devastating success against the Red Army. Blitzkrieg demanded total co-operation between the Wehrmacht's thrusting tank divisions on the ground and the Luftwaffe's dive-bomber units in the air. The panzers would make deep inroads into enemy territory without infantry support, which would only have slowed them up, and when they encountered a point of particularly strong resistance, they radioed in the Junkers Ju 87s to blast the opposition away for them. The dive-bombers acted, in effect, as long-range artillery and operated under the protection of fighter cover. Once the enemy had been cleared out of the panzers' path, they pushed forward again at high speed.

Experience in Spain had been useful, but Poland was the real testing ground.

Germany's campaign against Poland generally conjures up in most people's minds today pictures of vast fleets of Luftwaffe bombers indiscriminately razing Warsaw to the ground, fighters machine-gunning fleeing Polish cavalry and refugees, dive-bombers relentlessly frustrating attempted Polish counter-attacks. The truth, however, does not totally tally with the accepted picture.

The most generous estimate of the total number of aircraft the Reich could muster against Poland was 1,929, of which a mere 897 were bombers of all types. This contrasts strangely with the figure of 4,161 given in the official history, *The Royal Air Force 1939–45*. Against this the Poles could count on 159 fighters, 154 bombers and 84 reconnaissance aircraft. One-sided, yes, but not as much as is generally believed.

The war started at a quarter to five on the morning of 1 September 1939. As planned, the panzers rolled forward and began pushing the Poles back. But as time passed, Luftwaffe leaders began to worry. The Polish air force had not offered any resistance; where were they and what were they doing? Fighters escorting bomber formations kept a watchful eye open but in vain. Enemy airfields were bombed and straffed, runways were cratered, and hangers left blazing. Only after the campaign had been concluded did the Luftwaffe discover the Poles had realized that air attacks on their bases were inevitable and had pulled their machines and personnel back. For the main part the airfield attacks destroyed only obsolete types and trainers.

Over Warsaw, however, the Poles offered stiff resistance, Messerschmitt Bf 110s of I/L.G. 1 becoming entangled with thirty P.Z.L. 11c fighters. A second battle over the centre of the capital followed later when again some thirty Polish fighter aircraft attacked Luftwaffe fighters escorting the slower bombers. Spasmodic encounters then occurred in which, for example, elements of Bf 110-equipped Z.G. 76 met P.Z.L. 11cs over Lodz (destroying two Polish fighters but losing three of their own number) and I/Z.G. 2 equipped with Bf 109Ds later shot down eleven of the enemy over the same city. Polish bombers briefly succeeded in making their presence felt when they attacked panzer spearheads in the region of Radomsko but were quickly silenced by Luftwaffe fighters.

By the start of the second week, the Polish air force had to all intents and purposes been beaten. The Luftwaffe could then devote itself to supporting the panzers by reacting as swiftly as possible to their pleas for assistance. The most outstanding example followed the encircling of the still intact Polish 'Army of Posen' by the German IV, VIII, and X Armies. When the Poles, trying to break out by attacking the VIII Army to their south, breached the German lines at their first attempt, a dangerous situation rapidly built up and the Wehrmacht called for ground support missions to be flown. Henschel Hs 123 biplanes and Stukas responded by mounting concentrated low-level straffing attacks on the Polish Army, which soon lost its forward impetus. The Poles had been contained.

But continuing to battle bravely on, they refused to surrender, even when troops had been cut off from the River Vistula, behind which they had hoped to build up a renewed defence. The die was cast and Goering's 'Operation Seaside' was to go ahead. This envisaged a heavy bombing attack on Warsaw when it became obvious that its occupants had no intention of declaring it an open city.

Thought of by the outside world as the Second World War's first example of terror bombing the action was adamantly defended by those who planned the attack; only military targets in the city were to be hit. Even these were 'to be spared if situated in heavily populated city areas'. Orders from the Luftwaffe high command specifically stated 'Military targets only'. Public utilities,

ammunition dumps, barracks and the war ministry were among the targets detailed, but no authorisation was given for indiscriminate bombing of the city as a whole. No more than 400 horizontal and dive-bombers could have participated anyway, as the rest had been hastily bundled back to the west in case of Allied intervention. The plans went astray, however, and some 500 tons of high-explosive and 75 tons of incendiaries dropped on to the blazing city in what turned out to be a haphazard if not unplanned attack. The result was that Warsaw soon became enveloped by smoke, which consequently rendered any pinpoint bombing completely impossible.

The following day, 27 September, Poland capitulated.

Air versus Sea

Did war against Poland automatically mean war against Britain? Hitler hoped not, and in order not to fan the flames, prohibited the Luftwaffe from dropping bombs on British soil. On no account, it was decreed, should British civilian lives be lost through German aerial action. The British thought the same way and denied the R.A.F. the opportunity of striking land targets. Which, both sides reasoned, left only warships.

In their first attack of the war, the R.A.F. sent twin-engined Bristol Blenheim bombers to strike at the battleship *Admiral Scheer*, anchored in Schillig Roads. The attack failed; not because the bomb-aimers failed to score hits on their targets but because some of the bombs were duds! Wellington bombers were simultaneously launched against the *Gneisenau* and the *Scharnhorst* lying off Bruensbuttel, but the ships put up such a heavy curtain of fire that the attackers failed to penetrate it. The Luftwaffe scored its first victory against the new foe when Sgt Alfred Held of II J.G. 77, in his Messerschmitt Bf 109, shot down one of the Wellingtons.

The British were not the only ones to taste failure. Reconnaissance having located a British flotilla that included the battleships *Nelson* and

Rodney, the battle-cruisers *Hood* and *Renown*, and the aircraft-carrier *Ark Royal*, Heinkel He 111s of K.G. 26 and Junkers Ju 88s of the 'Eagle' *Geschwader* took off with full bomb loads. Corporal Carl Franke, diving his Ju 88 down against the *Ark Royal*, dropped two bombs, but though his crew reported that the second might have scored a possible hit on the carrier's bows, nobody was quite certain. Unfortunately for Franke, Goebbels's propaganda machine took over, and very soon the luckless aviator found himself a national hero. Goering even promoted and decorated him. The sad facts of the matter were that *Ark Royal* escaped unscathed and left for the south Atlantic to search for the *Admiral Graf Spee*.

Then, on 18 December 1939, there followed a raid that was to have an effect totally out of proportion to its actual scale. Wellington bombers of R.A.F. Squadrons 9, 37 and 149 set off on what the British later described as an 'armed reconnaissance' over the Heligoland Bight. The twenty-two Wellingtons (two having dropped out) were duly picked up on radar sets operated by the German Navy, and Luftwaffe fighters scrambled in large numbers. The slow twin-engined bombers fought back bravely, but their fate was sealed. Twelve were shot down and a further three so badly damaged that they broke up on making forced landings. The Messerschmitts had enjoyed a field day. The higher echelons of the R.A.F. realized that their maxim, 'the bomber will always get through', had been faulty and ruled that further attacks would be made under cover of night. Thus were planted the seeds of the British night offensive.

The invasion of Norway and Denmark was marked primarily, from the Luftwaffe's point of view, by the world's first use of paratroops. Additionally, the bombers distinguished themselves by neutralizing the British-French-Polish troops landed in Norway by destroying their supply ports.

After a short battle, the airborne troops, operating under fighter cover provided by I/Z.G. 76's Bf 110s, managed to take Oslo-Fornebu and make it a base from which to capture Norway's

capital. Stavanger-Sola on the south-west coast was taken after a brief thirty-minute battle in which parachutists threw hand grenades through the embrasures of two gun emplacements. German mastery of the air was never really challenged throughout the campaign, save for a brave effort by a handful of Norwegian pilots flying British Gloster Gladiator biplanes. Horizontal and dive-bombers struck at such strong points as fortresses, coastal batteries and flak positions, which were then rapidly taken from the air by parachutists. Paratroops, too, were responsible for capturing the important bridge linking the Danish islands of Falster and Zealand.

It was perhaps just as well that intensive bombing operations were not required, for the Scandinavians' token resistance meant aircraft were free to strike at the Royal Navy if it appeared: which it soon did. Eighty-eight twin-engined Heinkels and Junkers of the X Air Corps battered the flotilla for some three hours, scoring a direct hit with a 1,000 lb bomb on the battleship *Rodney*. The *Rodney*, however, was wisely equipped with extra armour-plating against aerial attack and the bombs failed to penetrate. Better luck attended the bombers' attacks against the cruisers *Devonshire*, *Southampton* and *Glasgow*, which were all damaged, and the destroyer *Gurkha*, which was sunk.

The tri-service Allied Expeditionary Force put ashore in central Norway between 14 and 19 April immediately made efforts to link up with Norwegian troops, but without sufficient air cover the Allies' task was impossible. British fighters had to operate either off aircraft carriers or from far away bases in Scotland. With the Luftwaffe supreme in the air and destroying the Allies' ports of supply unchallenged, the hopelessness of their situation was soon realized and they were taken off from the same ports at which they had landed.

Capturing keypoints
A droll sequel to the twin invasions was provided by Lieutenant Guenther Mehrens of *Kustenfliegergruppe* 706, which was equipped with single-engined Arado Ar 196 seaplanes. Mehrens had the good fortune to locate the British

submarine *Seal* just after she had struck a mine, and after a brief bombing attack he landed alongside her and called her captain to swim over. The captain, Lieutenant-Commander Robert Lonsdale, celebrated his thirty-fifth birthday in the back of the Arado's cockpit, being flown prisoner to the German-captured base of Aalborg. A fishing steamer later towed the *Seal* and its crew of sixty into captivity.

Although the invasion of Scandinavia marked the first employment of airborne paratroops, their most dramatic success was yet to come.

The Belgian fort of Eben Emael dominated all defence systems through which the German panzers would have to crash if they were to take the country. The fort itself consisted of a series of rotating cupolas containing guns up to 120 mm and protected on the ground by walls, anti-tank ditches, pillboxes and machine-gun positions. Anti-aircraft guns and attendant searchlight batteries were also provided, and two sides of the fort fell 120 feet in a sheer drop to the Albert Canal below. All emplacements were interconnected by underground tunnels.

It was evident to the German planners that a ground attack would either fail or incur extremely heavy losses. The armour-plating with which many of the emplacements were reinforced might even defeat pinpoint attacks by Junkers Ju 87 Stukas. There was only one way – Luftwaffe paratroops landed by glider actually on top of the fort itself, without warning. Taking maximum advantage of their unannounced arrival, they would then storm the emplacements and hold the fort until the infantry arrived. This was the task of a force of eighty-five specially trained men codenamed 'Granite'. Three other task forces, codenamed 'Concrete', 'Steel' and 'Iron', would simultaneously drop on the three key bridges of Vroenhoven, Veldwezelt and Kanne.

A total of forty-one tri-engined Junkers Ju 52 transport aircraft duly took off from airfields near Cologne at 4.30 a.m. on 10 May 1940, each one towing a glider packed full of paratroops and their weapons. From the start, however, things began to go awry. 'Granite' was headed by First-Lieutenant Witzig, a man whose presence

was vital to the success of the operation, but when the Ju 52 towing his glider prematurely released it, the glider pilot had no alternative but to sail back to Cologne. A short while later another glider was prematurely released. Worse still, the remaining transport aircraft did not give their release signals until the Belgians and Dutch had actually heard the engines of the approaching armada, whereupon anti-aircraft fire opened up immediately. By a miracle, though, the force got through and, finally, the gliders floated away from their parent aircraft. Sweeping silently out of the night, the gliders of 'Granite' force landed in rapid succession actually among the emplacements and the bewildered troops manning them.

The Germans sprang into action, placing 100 lb hollow-charges against the emplacements, throwing charges down barrels, and suppressing Belgian machine-gun fire. Right in the thick of it, First-Lieutenant Witzig arrived, having successfully found another towing aircraft. Soon, Heinkel He 111 bombers swooped in, dropping containers of extra ammunition and charges, and 'Granite' hung on grimly through the night until leading units of the army were sighted the following morning. It was virtually all over, and the fort's commander, Major Jottrand, decided to surrender.

The landings at Vroenhoven and Veldwezelt were also successful, both bridges being captured and held. The Belgian force defending the Kanne bridge had proved too speedy for the men of 'Iron' force, however, and had blown it sky high as the gliders touched down. Notwithstanding the Kanne catastrophe, the operation was all in all a real feather in the cap of the Luftwaffe's paratroopers.

Breaking Dutch resistance

The new weapon, sure enough, was proving effective in the extreme, and was to prove itself further during the invasion of the Netherlands. Once again, Luftwaffe paratroops were to descend from the sky and cause confusion and panic among defending ground troops. This time they were employed to capture airfields in The Hague area and an airfield and vital bridge in the Rotterdam region. Now, however, the Germans' tactics differed slightly because paratroop assaults on the airfields were in some cases preceded by bombing attacks carried out by K.G. 4 to soften up any resistance.

Undoubtedly the single feature of the Nazi invasion of the Netherlands that later caused most controversy was the bombing of Rotterdam. Rotterdam Old Town around the Maas river was quickly gutted by fire that killed some 900 civilians and seemed to symbolize to the Dutch people the futility of further resistance.

In fact, the whole attack was a nightmarish mistake. Paratroops of III/I.R.16 and sappers of II/Pi 22 were landed by seaplane on the Maas river, in the centre of the city, to capture and hold for later troops the important Willems bridge that spanned it. The defenders put up a stiff fight, and the Germans rapidly found themselves having to form a little enclave around the bridge, surrounded by hostile Dutchmen. To the commander of the Dutch troops, Colonel Scharroo, there was no earthly reason why he should order his men to surrender to the small German force holding the Willems bridge when they demanded that he do so. He did, however, enter into negotiations with them.

The German High Command, meanwhile, was impatient for a speedy surrender and ordered that resistance at Rotterdam should be broken 'by every means'. Conversely, it was also ordered that 'all means to prevent unnecessary bloodshed among the Dutch population' should be used. Parleys between the German and Dutch forces surrounding the bridge meandered on, the German commander stressing to his enemy counterpart that Rotterdam would be hit if his men did not surrender. But to Colonel Scharroo the German demand seemed unrealistic, surrounded as he was by his own men and confronted with only a tiny Nazi force.

The German leader, Lieutenant-Colonel Dietrich von Choltitz, sent a message to the Luftwaffe ordering the attack to be postponed 'owing to parley'. But events had overtaken both sides as 100 Heinkel He 111 bombers of K.G. 54 took off for Rotterdam and Choltitz's message failed to get through in time owing to bad radio frequencies. With the approach of the bombers, German officers rushed out into the middle of the streets and fired off red Very lights, the signal for the attack not to take place. But only part of the massive German formation saw the tiny lights burning far below them, and in the event fifty-seven released their bombs; forty-three did not. The result for Rotterdam, despite the desperate last-minute efforts to avert disaster, was terrible.

The battle against France
Now only France lay between the German dreams of hegemony of Europe and their realization.

The Allies entered the war under two severe disadvantages, and were aware of neither. Firstly, unknown to the Franco-British planners, Germany planned to attack through the Ardennes with large concentrated forces of panzers. (The densely forested Ardennes in north-east France were held by the Allies to be unsuitable terrain for tank operations; they were soon to discover differently.) Secondly, they were unaware of, and unprepared for, the new technique of warfare known as Blitzkrieg. Their thinking was dominated by the traditionalists and conservatives who looked back to the First World War and imagined the second conflict would assume the static trenchlike aspects of 1914–18.

Consequently, when Kleist's armoured divisions plunged into France between the towns of Sedan and Dinant in those historic first days of May 1940, the scene was all set for the greatest Allied debacle of the war. The armour was heavily covered by an umbrella of fighters and 'destroyers' (twin-engined long-range Messerschmitt Bf 110s) to ward off any possible intervention. Dive-bombers went ahead, attacking anticipated strongpoints of resistance and easing the tanks' forward passage.

There was no fighter with the performance of the Messerschmitt Bf 109 in large-scale service with the French Armée de l'Air at the time of the invasion. Their best was the Dewoitine D520 which, when it did come into contact with the German fighters, gave a good account of itself.

But the Moranes, Blochs and American-built Curtiss Hawks widely employed by the French made only a very little dent in the clouds of black-crossed fighters and bombers over their homeland. As for the British Expeditionary Force and their Spitfires and Hurricanes, it was basically a question of 'good equipment but inadequate in numbers'.

For the first time, however, really large air clashes did occur when French fighter units made determined attacks on German bombers *en route* to their targets lying in the path of the panzers. Luftwaffe fighter units quickly ran up large scores of kills, J.G. 3 claiming no less than 179 enemy aircraft and J.G. 2 a further 89 downed in combat. However, one of the Luftwaffe's brightest stars, Captain Werner Moelders, was shot down by a young French fighter pilot named Pommier-Layrargues flying a D520, though he was later liberated by German troops.

Once the Nazi armour had successfully broken through the Allies' light defensive screen, it streamed forward to the coast at high speed. Although this proved an excellent tactic, its single danger lay in the fact that both flanks would be fully exposed. Realizing this, French tank forces made a valiant attack at Arras, pressing their attacks home with determination and courage. But once again the Stukas had the last say. They harried Allied armoured columns without mercy, reducing their numbers so much that the remainder had no alternative but melt away, a broken, dispersed force.

And the British? They fared little better than the French. The new Bristol Blenheims of No. 140 Squadron were caught napping and were destroyed in their entirety on the ground by Dornier Do 17s of II/K.G. 2 led by Lieutenant-Colonel Paul Weitkus. Again, when the Wehrmacht captured bridges at Maastricht, vital to the advance of following units, the R.A.F. Blenheim and Battle medium- and light-bombers sent in to destroy them were nearly all lost. The Blenheims had the bad luck to be spotted by J.G. 1 and 27 and almost all were shot down, while the hapless Battles, despite being protected by Hurricane fighters, were slaughtered by heavy and accurate fire by flak. Hurricane units operated by the Belgians were also mauled by German fighter pilots, among them one Captain Adolf Galland.

Bit by bit, Allied ground units fell back on the small French port of Dunkirk. The story of their subsequent escape to England aboard ships of the Royal Navy, Channel steamers and a host of tiny privately owned boats has been recounted many times, but why did the victorious German Wehrmacht and Luftwaffe not prevent the khaki masses from embarking? The answer is two-fold. Firstly, Hitler at this point still hoped for some kind of settlement between the two countries and was, therefore, reluctant to score what would amount to a major victory over a potential neutral or even ally. Secondly, the Fuehrer was well aware that his tank units were tired after their headlong dash across northern France and needed time to rest and service their machines. Additionally, the bulk of France had still not been touched, and who knew what lay ahead of the panzers?

Goering, when he saw Hitler's predicament, entered the stage with one of his characteristically bombastic statements – let 'his' Luftwaffe deal with the soldiers on the beaches. Hitler gave the Reichsmarshal *carte blanche* and, accordingly, ordered the advancing panzers to halt in the green fields just outside the small port. But here the elements intruded; of the nine days it took to lift the troops off the beach, only two and a half of them were suitable flying days. A further drawback was that the sand tended to 'swallow' the force of bomb explosions. When the weather lifted, however, the omnipresent Stukas took their usual toll, concentrating their attacks against the largest vessels they could find in Dunkirk harbour and sinking a considerable number of troop-festooned Channel steamers and Royal Navy destroyers. Nevertheless, attack from the air proved to be entirely the wrong approach to this type of problem, and further setbacks were suffered at the hands of R.A.F. Spitfires and Hurricanes operating from bases in south-east England. The Stukas were particularly vulnerable.

So it was that no less than 338,226 men boarded the weird collection of vessels and managed to sail to England and safety.

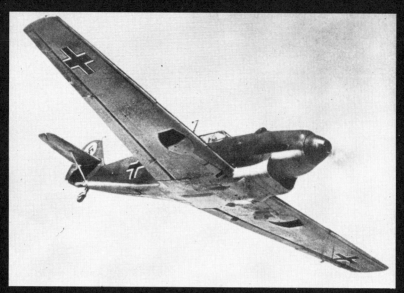

Eagles Over England

From the narrow London streets of 1940 a Cockney could hardly hear the stutter of cannon and machine-gun fire above him. As myriads of sunlit silver dots twisted and dived through the blue summer sky, he could not realize that history was being written.

Later, when the tremors created by the world's second shattering conflict in less than half a century had subsided, mankind came to regard the Battle of Britain as one of the most decisive ever fought. The victory won by British fighter pilots against the Luftwaffe guaranteed, if not final victory, at least the country's continued survival and liberty. And the events of that glorious summer, now slipped into history, prompted Winston Churchill, on 20 August 1940, to say: 'Never in the field of human conflict was so much owed by so many to so few.'

But was it really a question of 'so few'? And if it was, why then did the Luftwaffe fail to destroy Fighter Command? Why, in essence, did the German air offensive against Britain as a prelude to invasion not succeed?

Right from the start of the Battle, the Luftwaffe operated under a number of severe disadvantages. Firstly, the single-seat single-engined Messerschmitt Bf 109s were forced to fight at the absolute limits of their range which meant that their combat time over target was also limited. The further the target from their bases in France, the fewer the precious minutes during which they could engage R.A.F. Hurricanes and Spitfires in dogfights. Since the primary purpose of the offensive was to destroy the British fighter force, this inability to enter sustained combat represented a disastrous handicap.

When air fighting occurred over the Channel, both sides would race to the aid of pilots shot down 'in the drink' and floating either by virtue of their Mae Wests (in the case of the R.A.F.) or in their rubber dinghies (in the case of the Luftwaffe). But German pilots forced to bale out over England were promptly taken prisoner and so prevented from re-entering the Battle.

A further frustration to German aims was the British lead in the field of radar. Although it has, in the past, been popularly suggested that the Luftwaffe did not possess radar at all, it was, in 1940, operating two types, known as 'Freya' and 'Wuerzburg'. Freya was in wider use than its partner and was employed, among other tasks, to locate Channel convoys which would then be subject to aerial attack. The British lead lay primarily in the field of organization. A string of radar stations had been established on the southern coast, and this 'looked' out over the Channel and northern France to record air movements and any build-up of large formations. Information gained by the stations was then flashed to R.A.F. operations rooms where a complete picture of air activity was established and progressively updated as new data became available. Fighter controllers were thus ideally situated to assess where threats lay, how strong the German formations were, and which R.A.F. squadrons were best placed to effect interceptions. No equivalent organization existed in Germany, nor in German-occupied Europe, and the British lead in this field was a very real and meaningful achievement.

As if this was not enough, it was soon discovered that the performance of the two-seat twin-engined Messerschmitt Bf 110 was totally inadequate to enter combat with the faster, more nimble British fighters on anything like equal terms. (See section on this aircraft.) Although the 'one-one-oh' possessed the range so sadly lacking in the 'one-oh-nine', it proved far too cumbersome and large for dogfighting. This imposed the ludicrous necessity on the Bf 109s of having to defend their twin-engined colleagues.

Enter Churchill. A detester of red-tape himself, Churchill recognized a similar quality in the Press baron, Lord Beaverbrook, and promptly made him Minister of Aircraft Production. The latter rated fighter production his highest priority and performed a miracle in meeting his promise to the Prime Minister that he would replace losses incurred throughout the Battle as they happened. Under his energetic leadership, factories began producing Hurricanes and Spitfires by the hundred; in June their output had reached approximately 450 a month. Equivalent German fighter production figures do not tell the same happy tale, however. In June, a mere 164 were delivered to fighter units, and in July just over 200. The British lead meant that when their pilots bailed out and landed, within hours they could be back in the cockpit again.

Beaverbrook's success also had further unpleasant repercussions for the enemy. It meant that the R.A.F.'s actual fighter strength did not really decline throughout the Battle. It started at about 700 Hurricanes and Spitfires and ended at about 700. But because German factories were producing aircraft at a far more sluggish rate, German fighter strength did decline as losses sustained began to mount. Nor did the Luftwaffe enter the Battle with anything like the superior numbers of single-engined fighters generally accepted; they, too, were equipped with about 700 single-engined fighters (734) at the outset of the Battle, all of them Bf 109s. True they possessed additional fighters in the form of 268 Bf 110s but, as already mentioned, this type proved to be a calamitous failure in the bomber escort role.

And what of the bombers themselves? They were all twin-engined types! Not one four-engined strategic bomber dropped its weapon load on this country throughout the entire Battle. This, of course, reflected the low priority given to the design and production of four-engined types after the death of General Wever, but it was only when equipped in later years with such four-engined types as the Halifax, Stirling and Lancaster that R.A.F. Bomber Command inflicted such heavy damage on numerous German cities. How then did the Luftwaffe hope to bring Britain to her knees if this key type of aircraft was missing from its inventory? Faulty planning had struck at the vitals of the Luftwaffe and deprived it of an important weapon, just when that weapon was most needed.

Probably the greatest disadvantage under which the German fliers had to labour was the changeability of their own leadership. The course of history might well have been changed had Goering stuck to his guns and allowed the Luftwaffe to attack one specific type of target through thick and thin. But he did not. No sooner had the German bombers started to make some

genuine impression on a certain category of target than Goering would switch emphasis to another kind. The outstanding example was the series of attacks on airfields in southern England in which severe damage was inflicted on many and the whole machinery of Fighter Command was strained to its limits. Yet as soon as the Luftwaffe succeeded in inflicting what could have become mortal wounds on the ring of defensive fighter stations around London had the attacks continued, Goering gave this up and reallocated his priorities.

It is only against a background featuring these crucial points that an account of the Battle from the German viewpoint can be seen in a true perspective.

The opening stages

If 'Operation Sealion', Hitler's projected invasion of Great Britain, were to take place, then it was essential that the Channel be cleared of British shipping, both merchant vessels and those of the Royal Navy. Accordingly, on 10 July, some seventy bombers and fighters took off to attack a convoy steaming peacefully without protection. Hurricanes and Spitfires of four squadrons were duly scrambled and the first of many large-scale dogfights ensued, the fighters cavorting like gnats above the ships, twisting and turning to gain advantage on each other. Although the Luftwaffe lost four aircraft to the R.A.F.'s three, the important thing was that the convoy lost only one small vessel and sailed on virtually intact.

The following day the Luftwaffe returned, this time to strike at a convoy in the Lyme Bay region. Although nine R.A.F. fighters took off to counter the threat, they found themselves outnumbered seven to one, a situation that resulted in the rapid loss of three of them in return for a single Stuka. But, once again, the convoy escaped unscathed.

Although attacks continued day by day, no real success was registered until 25 July, on which date sixty Luftwaffe bombers with fighter escort dived on a convoy of twenty-one merchant ships and speedily sank five. A further half-dozen were severely damaged and, to add insult to injury, high speed E-boats emerged from their French ports under cover of night to despatch three of them. Two days later two destroyers from Dover went to the bottom under the weight of German bombs and a couple of days later a third was sunk. The remaining destroyers retired to safer Portsmouth.

The Germans then constructed a radar station at Wissant, almost opposite Dover, to detect movements in the Channel. On 8 August it picked up twenty-five merchant ships hoping to slip up the Channel under darkness. This time the convoy was accompanied by anti-aircraft destroyers of the Royal Navy. First blood went to the E-boats when they sank three and damaged a couple more, but the Luftwaffe followed hard on their heels, large formations of Stukas escorted by fighters appearing in the vicinity of the Isle of Wight. No less than seven squadrons of R.A.F. fighters offered combat, and once again large dogfights ensued, the British attempting to penetrate the screen of Bf 109s to get at the Stukas behind. At the end of the furious engagement, thirty-one Luftwaffe aircraft had been destroyed for the loss of nineteen British. The convoy lost three vessels.

An interesting aside occurred in July which spelled the death of the single-engined Defiant as a day fighter. Produced by Boulton Paul, this unusual machine looked exactly like a fighter of the Spitfire-Messerschmitt Bf 109 variety except for a large bomber-style turret just behind the cockpit. Unfortunately for the R.A.F., the gun turret imposed a heavy penalty on the type's performance, and once Luftwaffe fighter pilots had learned to avoid its fire they rapidly took a heavy toll. The Defiant was finally withdrawn from day combat after a disastrous incident on 19 July when Bf 109s shot down five from a formation of six and forced the sixth to crash land.

In August, the Luftwaffe were given another target: the coastal radar stations. Without their radar 'eyes', it was reasoned, R.A.F. fighters would be powerless to position themselves in the paths of the incoming German formations. Take out the radar stations, therefore, and this problem would be solved. And so early August saw heavy bombing attacks against the British coastal radar chain. The attacking aircrew were soon disappointed, however. The flimsy-looking aerial masts simply refused to collapse. All associated buildings, such as transmitting and receiving blocks, proved easy to pulverize, but the force of the explosions harmlessly carried right through the lattice-work of a mast itself. Limited success was experienced when Messerschmitt Bf 110s of Experimental Gruppe 210 put Pevensey off the air and severely hit Rye and Dover on 12 August, and the same day better luck attended attacks by K.G. 51 and 54 when they blasted the radar station at Ventnor, putting it out of action for eleven days. The others, however, were all functioning within a few hours of the attacks.

Disillusioned, Goering ordered the weight of the attacks to be switched to fighter airfields. The Hurricanes and Spitfires would be drawn into conflict and so destroyed by defending their own bases.

In rapid succession the airfields of Lympne, Manston and Hawkinge were struck by a total of some 300 bombers and dive-bombers. The radar station covering Manston had been silenced and, as a result, bomb-carrying Bf 110s of *Experimental Gruppe* 210 found themselves over their target just as the first wave of No. 65 Squadron's Spitfires clawed into the air. Four of the Spitfires were instantly downed and a further five aircraft destroyed on the ground. Hangars and vital installations were reduced to rubble. Hawkinge and Lympne similarly suffered.

The battle reaches a climax

A new tactic was then tried. Twenty-three Bf 110s of V.(Z.)/L.G. 1 took off to try deliberately to attract the attentions of defending R.A.F. fighters, thus hopefully leaving the air clear for following waves of bombers. With three Hurricane and Spitfire squadrons scrambled to intercept them, it seemed at first that the idea was going to work. But disaster struck when five of the Bf 110s were shot down and the bombers were no less than three hours late, which gave defending fighters ample time to land, rearm and refuel.

Air activity remained at peak level. Stukas of St.G. 77, escorted by Bf 109s of J.G. 27, took off to hit airfields in the Portland area. Some seventy British fighters intercepted the force, and the Hurricanes succeeded in engaging the Bf 109s so heavily that the Spitfires were left free to concentrate on the unfortunate Ju 87s, five of which were soon shot down.

After minor attacks on Middle Wallop and Andover, Bf 109s later cleared the way for Stukas to attack Detling near Maidstone, although it was not a fighter base (it belonged to Coastal Command). The Stukas destroyed hangars, runways, some twenty aircraft on the ground, and the operations room. Because of bad weather, only one attack was made on 14 August, this by Bf 110s against Manston. Their achieved surprise left four hangars burning. The weather improved the following afternoon and accordingly two *Gruppen* of Stukas with fighter escort again attacked Lympne and Hawkinge. As a result the former was knocked out for a further two days.

Catastrophe attended attacks made by the Norwegian based *Luftflotte* 5 when they sent two whole *Geschwader* of Heinkel He 111s and Junkers Ju 88s to hit targets between the Tyne and Humber rivers. Spitfires of No. 72 and 79 Squadrons made mincemeat of the escorting Bf 110 fighters and thoroughly broke up the Heinkels' attack, forcing them to jettison their bombs over a wide area. The Junkers managed to get through, however, and bombed Driffield, a bomber base.

R.A.F. fighter controllers began to find their plotting boards swamped with fixes when three *Gruppen* of K.G. 3 (Dornier Do 17s) and *Gruppen* of Bf 109-equipped J.G. 26, 51, 52 and 54 all flew simultaneously over southern England on 15 August. Although eleven R.A.F. squadrons took off, they were obliged to dart here and there in small numbers and so failed to make any major impression on the attackers. Stations at Martlesham and Eastchurch, and factories at Rochester producing the four-engined Stirling bomber were severely hit, especially the factories, which ended up gutted. A few hours later some 200 more German aircraft of all types were again heading for southern England, and large dogfights

ensued. Junkers Ju 88s hit the totally unprepared R.A.F. Middle Wallop hard and wiped out in a flash the better part of two squadrons on the ground. Faulty navigation on the part of some German bomber crews resulted in a lucky break for Fighter Command bases when Croydon and West Malling were hit during a following raid instead of the planned targets of Kenley and Biggin Hill.

The following day, 16 August, R.A.F. West Malling was again struck and remained unoperational for the following days. Fourteen R.A.F. aircraft were later destroyed when Stukas of St.G. 2 and Ju 88s of K.G. 51 blasted Tangmere. The British, however, continued to take a heavy toll, especially when they found the Stukas bereft of protection or could manage to penetrate German fighter screens to get at the bombers 'hiding' behind.

After a day of little activity on the seventeenth, things hotted up again on the eighteenth when K.G.76 hit Kenley, setting hangars on fire, pitting the runway, and knocking out the operations room. The demise of the Stuka took place on this day, however, when Spitfires of No. 152 Squadron and Hurricanes of No. 43 Squadron found four *Gruppen* of the dive-bombers attacking airfields and radar stations on the south coast. The fighters waded in and shot them down in droves; I/St.G. 77 lost twelve of its twenty-eight aircraft within minutes, and altogether thirty Stukas were destroyed during that single engagement. The Junkers Ju 87 was then withdrawn from the Battle.

Operations continued at such a pace that by 24 August it was questionable for how much longer the ring of fighter stations protecting the capital could hold out against further attacks. On the night of the twenty-fourth, though, something happened that would shape the course of the future air war. A small number of German bombers made a fateful mistake and offloaded their bombs on the City of London, thereby sparking off a furious call from Churchill for a raid of revenge on Berlin. And on the night of 25–26 August, twin-engined Wellingtons, Hampdens, and Whitleys duly carried out the

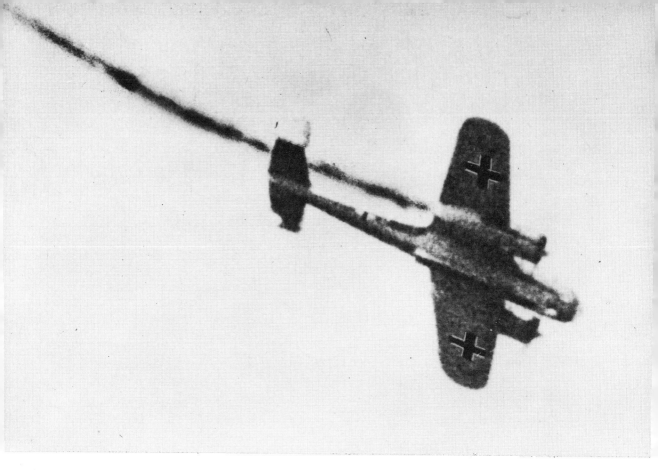

attacks on the Third Reich's capital. This, in turn, smouldered in Hitler's mind and undoubtedly helped frame his decision to switch the attack to London later on.

Meanwhile, however, the series of strikes against British air bases were to continue. On the morning of 31 August, Debden and Eastchurch were both hit, after which Detling was straffed by Bf 109s of I/J.G. 52. With R.A.F. operations rooms once again becoming saturated by incoming attacks, the alert at Hornchurch was not given until K.G. 2's Dorniers were actually over the airfield. Fighter pilots hauled their Spitfires off the runway with Luftwaffe bombs bursting all around them!

Because of the undiminished opposition, it was decided to mount yet another attack on the vital base of Biggin Hill. The Kent base had been struck three times on the thirtieth, and it was hoped the thirty-first would finally witness the demise of this key station, the home of newly-arrived No. 72 Squadron (Spitfires) and No. 79 Squadron (Hurricanes). With both squadrons engaged further south, K.G. 2 found itself unopposed and obliterated hangars, workshops, billets, runways and the operations room. Biggin Hill pilots, temporarily, had to be controlled from Kenley.

At this point bomber pilots began to report less trouble than usual from defending fighters. The R.A.F. lost 390 Hurricanes and Spitfires during August, while the Luftwaffe lost 231 Bf 109s. The Luftwaffe, therefore, was shooting down more R.A.F. single-seat fighters than the R.A.F. was Luftwaffe single-seaters. It should be borne in mind, though, that the R.A.F. was also hacking its way through to the German bombers with reasonable success and destroying numbers of these as well. Could it be, however, that Fighter Command had been, if not knocked out, at least winded?

Air Marshal Dowding was to write later that the rate of R.A.F. loss was so high that fresh squadrons moved down from the north were exhausted before convalescing squadrons just moved up there were fully prepared to return to the south themselves. Another problem facing the R.A.F. concerned new pilots. Although Beaverbrook's efforts meant aircraft could be replaced, pilots under training were short.

Just when it looked as though the Luftwaffe

114

might be on the brink of gaining air supremacy, Hitler and Goering stepped in and made their fatal pronouncement. From now on the target would be London itself. Just as he had changed from shipping to radar stations, and from radar stations to airfields, so Goering was now going to allow the Fuehrer to make a switch of his own; from airfields to the capital city.

Target London

And so 7 September saw the first heavy raid on London carried out by 625 bombers and 648 single- and twin-engined fighters. From the Luftwaffe's point of view at least, the change of target gave them the advantage of catching Fighter Command unawares; the German formations arrived over London intact. The docks burned furiously and acted as a beacon for further bombers flying in at night.

A week later, on 15 September, heavy fighting raged once again over the skies of southern England. With some 300 Hurricanes and Spitfires in the air simultaneously, the Luftwaffe had to hammer its way through to London against furious opposition. Although Churchill's claim of 185 aircraft downed that day was far in excess of the actual figure of 56, the correct statistic was serious enough, for it meant that about one quarter of the bombers were *hors de combat*. Obviously the Hurricanes and Spitfires were not being destroyed in sufficient numbers and Fighter Command was still very far from being neutralized. The realization that one huge 'knockout' blow was no longer feasible, combined with the deterioration of the weather, rapidly led to a reduction and finally to a collapse of the Luftwaffe's daylight raid plans. Although further sorties were made by bomb-carrying Bf 109s during daylight hours, large scale raids were now to be made at night. The 'Blitz' had been born.

Everybody knows the story of how Londoners endured Goering's nocturnal attacks. With dogged determination and a rough and ready humour, they coined the phrase 'London can take it' and carried on as well as they could. It seemed to the inhabitants of London to be the time of their greatest test but, in fact, the period of critical danger for the country as a whole had now passed. Invasion was no longer possible. Although from November the inhabitants of other major cities such as Liverpool, Manchester, Southampton and Plymouth were also to feel the effects of German night attacks, owing to another target switch, the severity of the blows was diminishing month by month. The total tonnage of bombs dropped in November was just under six and a quarter thousand; in December this dropped to just over four and a quarter thousand, and in January a further decline reduced the tonnage to under two and a half thousand. In February a puny 1,000 tons were offloaded against the industrial cities of Britain. The night attacks petered out because the Luftwaffe was tired and needed to rest.

Perhaps one raid should be singled out for mention. How was it that the Heinkel He 111H-3s and their crews of K.G. 100 found and struck Coventry with such success during the night of 14 November?

The secret lay in a piece of radio-direction beam equipment named 'X Apparatus' carried in each aircraft. This picked up three concentrated radio beams laid across England by transmitting stations on the French coast. The Heinkels flew along the first beam until they arrived at a second that intersected it at slightly less than a right angle, whereupon a crew member set the first hand of a special clock in the aircraft in motion. The aircraft was then twelve miles from target and on course. At six miles from target the aircraft encountered a third beam, which meant the first hand stopped and a second started. The pilot then maintained altitude, speed and course until the second hand completed its revolution, made an electrical contact, and released the bomb load. Once K.G. 100 had started sufficient fires to mark the fated town, following units totalling 449 bombers dropped some 500 tons of high explosive and 30 tons of incendiary bombs plumb on target.

Unfortunately for the Germans, however, it was to be left to Bomber Command in following years to bring the art of nocturnal bombing by means of radio devices to its most sophisticated pitch. They followed, and improved on, the lead given by K.G. 100 over Coventry that terrible night.

Sand and Snow

When Mussolini's invasion of Greece on 28 October 1940 stalled at its first attempt and the British, already in Greece, also promptly occupied Crete the following day, Hitler began to fear for the safety of his vitally important oilfields in Romania, which had now fallen within the range of R.A.F. four-engined bombers. And with preparations for 'Operation Barbarossa', the invasion of the U.S.S.R., now well advanced, the Fuehrer could not risk an uncertain situation on what would become his southern flank.

A lightning attack against Yugoslavia and Greece on 6 April 1941 rapidly brought German troops to the Aegean and Mediterranean coastlines, forcing Greece to capitulate on 21 April and the remaining British troops to retreat from the mainland to join their colleagues already on the small but strategically placed island of Crete.

Paratroops had cracked several hard nuts during the European campaigns, and now the men of the XI Air Corps, consisting of one paratroop and one airborne division, were given the opportunity of proving their worth once again during 'Operation Mercury', the capture of Crete.

Launched on 20 May, the operation promptly ran into trouble. Aerial reconnaissance photographs taken previously by the Luftwaffe had failed to show how deeply entrenched the British, New Zealanders, Australians and Greeks really were. Despite softening up attacks by Dornier and Heinkel bombers of K.G. 2 and 26, numerous Stuka attacks, and straffing by Bf 109s and Bf 110s of J.G. 77 and Z.G. 26, the initial droppings were pinned to the ground under intense defensive fire. In many cases the Germans were even unable to reach their weapon containers to fight back. Of the 600 paratroops of the III Battalion, for example, nearly 400 were killed and other units were obliged to cling helplessly to the ground until reinforcements arrived. The 42,000 Allied troops fought with fanatical ferocity and for a long while the issue was in doubt.

The rudimentary Greek airfields from which the large force of tri-motor Junkers Ju 52 transport aircraft flew also created problems. Massive dust clouds rose from them at every take-off, so preventing crews from joining up into effective

numbers once airborne. The second wave of Ju
52s consequently flew to Crete and back in myriad
tiny groups, even singly and in pairs, which
prevented any concentrated large-scale droppings.

Obviously some kind of telling blow to swing
the battle in the Germans' favour was necessary,
but what? It was decided to take Malemes airfield
in the west of the 150 mile long island as soon
as possible, for once this was in German hands,
reinforcements could gain access to the island
interior from there.

So, during the afternoon of the battle's second
day, Ju 52 after Ju 52 swept in to land directly
under enemy fire. Men of the Mountain Division
leapt from their aircraft right in the face of
artillery and rifle fire, and gradually, through
pressure of sheer numbers, the Germans began
to gain the upper hand. Some 240 Ju 52s landed,
of which about one-third was destroyed on
touching down on the shell-pitted runway. The
scene resembled Dante's *Inferno* with blazing
aircraft at all angles on and around the strip itself,
attackers and defenders locked in combat, shells
falling thick and fast, and new aircraft setting
themselves down precariously amid the overall
chaos. Yet this daring attack was eventually to
win the Battle of Crete for the Germans,
establishing a firm toehold on the sun-drenched
island through which more troops were to be
poured.

Seen overall, however, 'Operation Mercury' was
a success that cost the Third Reich, and the
Luftwaffe in particular, very dear. Of the 22,000
men of the XI Air Corps taking part, no fewer
than 6,453 were killed, missing or wounded, and
a shockingly high total of 271 Ju 52s destroyed,
some 80 of them during the Malemes airfield
attack alone. These aircraft would be sorely
missed when Hitler ordered the VI Army
surrounded at Stalingrad to hold on and await
supplies from the air. Crete proved the graveyard
of the Luftwaffe's transport force and, in a very
real sense, also that of the German paratroop arm,
for never again in the war was it used for a
large-scale operation.

Having contributed decisively to the downfall
of the Allied troops holding Crete, the Luftwaffe

now humbled the Royal Navy. Two large British
forces had been spotted, one to the west of the
island and the other to the north, the latter
obviously intent on intercepting any German
seaborne reinforcements bound for Crete from
Greece, and destroying them. The alert was
instantly signalled to bomber, Stuka and fighter
units of the VIII Air Corps, stationed on the
Greek mainland, which immediately took off to
locate and attack the British Mediterranean Fleet.
Once found, the Fleet was subject to more or
less continuous attack by the German aircrew,
who flew a sort of bomber taxi service to and
fro between their bases and hapless victims. The
result for the Royal Navy was disastrous. The
destroyers *Juno*, *Greyhound*, *Kashmir*, *Kelly*,
Imperial and *Hereward*, and the cruisers
Gloucester, *Fiji* and *Calcutta* were all sunk. A
further three battleships, one aircraft carrier, seven
cruisers and four destroyers were all heavily or
slightly damaged. The Navy retired.

With the occupation of Yugoslavia, Greece and
Crete, the time was ripe for the grand onslaught
against Soviet Russia. And at exactly 3.15 a.m.
on 22 June 1941 the blow fell. Hitler had
proclaimed, 'We have only to kick in the front
door and the whole rotten edifice will come
tumbling down!' And at first it looked as though
he was right once again.

The Reich attacks Russia

For the Luftwaffe the first day of the war against
Russia was supremely successful. No less than
1,811 Soviet aircraft were destroyed on the ground
and in the air by fighters and flak for the trifling
loss in return of a mere thirty-five. The Russians
themselves later admitted to a loss of 1,200 before
noon. Everywhere it was the same story;
uncamouflaged Soviet machines were lined up on
their airfields as if ready for inspection. With the
air clear of enemy fighters, Luftwaffe bombers
swept in and showered fragmentation bombs
among them. The destruction was colossal.

Before the campaign was launched, Luftwaffe
leaders reckoned they faced a foe at least twice
as strong in numbers as they were themselves.
Indeed, the Germans fielded almost 2,000 aircraft

of which, however, only some 1,250 were actually serviceable. Had they known the truth their hair would have stood on end for, in fact, the Russians produced almost 16,000 aircraft of all types during 1941 alone! Terrific impetus had been placed behind increasing aircraft production and the rate of turn-out of some types had subsequently been trebled or even quadrupled.

Although the Luftwaffe was therefore outnumbered by frighteningly high odds, fortunately it was not merely numerical supremacy that counted. Tactics, the quality of aircraft, and training of aircrew were also vital considerations, and in these respects the Luftwaffe won hands down.

Notwithstanding the swingeing losses suffered by the Soviet Air Force, they were soon able to mount bomber attacks of retaliation against their former bases now under German control. Their tactics, however, were completely devoid of imagination. With no fighter protection, the Russian aircrew flew straight in to the attack in squadron strength, making no real attempt to avoid German fighters or flak, and their attacks, brave but futile, betrayed the lack of modern training they had received.

As in the European campaigns of the previous year, the Luftwaffe was called on to perform two main tasks: gain absolute ascendancy in the air and support Wehrmacht units on the ground. It was 'Blitzkrieg 1940-style' all over again. And once again it worked as Hitler's now unleashed Panzer formations pierced lines of opposition on the frontier and headed swiftly into the hinterland. Under an aerial umbrella of fighters, Stukas blasted away points of resistance, and within a very short time the Wehrmacht was putting its first objectives behind it and preparing for the campaign's initial encircling movements.

By 15 July the combined efforts of the Wehrmacht and Luftwaffe enabled the breakthrough in the centre that led to the encirclement and fall of Smolensk: 300,000 Russian troops were cut off and forced, on 5 August, to surrender. In mid-August the Wehrmacht advanced on Leningrad, and one month later Panzer spearheads under Kleist and

Guderian met at Lokhvitsa, trapping four Soviet armies in the Kiev area. By 27 September, almost two-thirds of the Red Army's strength at the outbreak of war had already been eliminated.

Now it was the turn of the Red Navy to feel the wrath of the Luftwaffe. On 23 September, Stukas of I and III/St.G. 2 dived on the Russian Baltic Fleet at anchor in Kronstadt and Leningrad. For the following four days they hammered home their attacks and reaped a rich reward, damaging a large number of destroyers and the heavy cruiser *Kirov*, and sinking the battleship *Marat*.

Then things began to go wrong for the invaders. To their dismay, Wehrmacht units began meeting new Soviet tanks, Russian resistance stiffened along the whole front, and the Russian Air Force soon showed itself far from neutralized. But, worst of all, the mud of autumn soon gave way to the blinding snow and thick ice of winter. The ratio of serviceable aircraft rapidly tumbled catastrophically as cases of frostbite among mechanics soared. Metal soon became impossible to touch without injury, and constant problems were experienced in preventing fuel and oil from freezing.

To make things worse, the Soviets were transferring their aircraft and tank-producing factories eastwards, out of range of the twin-engined Luftwaffe bombers. If Germany had possessed a four-engined bomber she would have been capable of destroying them, but once again the lack of such a weapon was to be decisive.

And then, on top of these setbacks, it was learned that the Japanese had struck without warning against the American fleet at Pearl Harbour. The following day, 7 December 1941, the United States of America was formally at war with the Land of the Rising Sun, to which Germany was allied in the Axis Pact. The Third Reich swiftly found itself saddled with a new foe and one, in addition, that was probably the most powerful country in the world.

Although events in the long-term looked full of shadows for Germany's air arm, short-term prospects were still much rosier. With the introduction into service in 1941 of the new radial-engined Focke Wulf Fw 190 fighter, the Luftwaffe at last found a truly superlative machine and one that had the Spitfire V outperformed for two whole years on the Channel front.

It was on the Channel front, too, that Germany's air force and navy now conspired to make the British look fools by slipping three capital ships, *Scharnhorst*, *Gneisenau* and *Prinz Eugen*, up the Channel from Brest to northern home waters. The ships would pass within less than twenty miles of the English coast and were accordingly provided aerial cover by no fewer than 252 Bf 109s and Fw 190s maintaining a constant umbrella of patrols over the valuable 30,000 ton vessels. When the British finally recognized what was happening, six Fleet Air Arm Swordfish torpedo biplanes lumbered into the attack but were all destroyed either by fighters or by the ships' anti-aircraft fire. R.A.F. Bomber Command later flung 242 bombers into the holocaust but, for the loss of fifteen of their number, none registered a hit. Even Fighter Command felt obliged to have a crack and threw in cannon-firing Hurricanes and Whirlwinds, which was something like trying to knock a house down with a teaspoon. The awesome trio steamed on intact to their destination and were not stopped even by later collisions with mines.

The Mediterranean theatre

While the Fuehrer's mind was obsessed with the mammoth struggle being acted out in the east, events on a smaller scale in the Mediterranean were slowly reaching a climax. Successful prosecution by Rommel and his Afrika Korps of the 'pendulum war' that swung to and fro across North Africa depended on his obtaining supplies of all kinds in bulk. But if German and Italian convoys were exposed to harassment by Allied naval or air forces, he could be starved of vital equipment, food, fuel, oil or munitions just when he most needed them. The tiny island of Malta sat fairly and squarely astride Rommel's extended and tenuous supply line and, therefore, had to be reduced to impotence or actually occupied.

Throughout the summer of 1941 Malta stocked up with supplies. R.A.F. aircraft flew in for

defence and the Royal Navy established a base from which to operate submarines, cruisers and destroyers. The effects began to be felt by Axis convoys plying between Italy and North Africa in September 1941, when shipping losses of some thirty-seven per cent were recorded. And then, in November, two British cruisers and two destroyers made a nocturnal interception of an Italian convoy of seven vessels and sank the lot within minutes. As a result, Rommel's proposed offensive that autumn had to be shelved, and it instantly became that much more imperative that Malta be subdued.

Over three hundred Ju 88s, Stukas, Bf 110s and Bf 109s were flown into Sicily to do the job. In March 1942 the period of Malta's most severe trial began. The total tonnage of bombs dropped on the island almost equalled that offloaded over southern England at the height of the Battle of Britain. Everything the Luftwaffe found they flattened; quays, harbour installations, airfields and a good deal of the town of Valletta all went the same way. But the British proved their determination to hang on to the bitter end by flying almost fifty new Spitfires into the besieged island from the American aircraft-carrier *Wasp*. Unfortunately for them, German radio monitoring experts were listening in to what was going on and soon calculated the fighters' arrival time. No sooner had the Spitfires landed than Luftwaffe bombers appeared over their airfield and knocked out twenty right away. The remainder was gradually reduced through facing superior odds.

The Axis increased its hold on Malta by forcing British warships and submarines to vacate Valletta harbour through heavy bombing. Obviously the Royal Navy could not risk losing vessels at anchor to aerial attacks. Luftwaffe bombers continued to take a heavy toll of any courageous Allied convoy that attempted to run their gauntlet into the harbour. On the other hand, more Axis convoys than ever were reaching Rommel intact with the much needed supplies for his Afrika Korps. Things were looking brighter for 'The Desert Fox'.

With Malta flattened and Rommel re-equipped, now was the time to put 'Operation Hercules' into action and invade the island, Crete-style, from the air. But though the project was often presented to Hitler as absolutely necessary, and it was frequently stressed that General Kurt Student and his XI Air Corps were simply awaiting their leader's word, the Fuehrer evaded the crucial issue and procrastinated endlessly. He preferred to leave the job to the Italians.

Four British destroyers, meanwhile, were engaged in a brave attempt to steam from the North African port of Alexandria and intercept Italian convoys supplying Rommel through Benghazi. However, they were spotted by a Luftwaffe reconnaissance aircraft and soon fell foul of L.G. 1's Junkers Ju 88s operating from Herakleion in Crete and Eleusis in Greece. If, after the 'Crete affair', further proof of the superiority of aircraft over ships in air-surface warfare was needed, the Luftwaffe now provided it once again. Three of the four destroyers, *Lively*, *Kipling* and *Jackal*, were swiftly sunk, leaving only *Jervis* to limp back to Alexandria on her own. The British sortie had accomplished nothing and suffered heavy loss.

On 10 May 1941, the Luftwaffe informed Hitler, 'Enemy naval and air bases at Malta eliminated'. But even as the signal reached the German leader, events started to prove precisely the opposite. The British had built bomb-proof shelters for aircraft and had been able to save some fuel and ammunition so that, when more than sixty Spitfires landed on the island from the aircraft carriers *Wasp* and *Eagle*, they were saved from the fate that befell the previous British eight-gun fighters. Additionally, new stocks of anti-aircraft shells were rushed into Malta by the fast minelayer *Welshman*. Just as Malta took on a new lease of life, so Hitler, convinced she was in her death throes, ordered Luftwaffe units in the area to aid hard-pressed Wehrmacht forces elsewhere. Some went to North Africa to support Rommel, some to the eastern front, which was now consuming men and material at an alarmingly high rate. With the dispersal of the German air units, Malta now rearmed as speedily as she could and soon became the old thorn in the side of Rommel's supply lines she had previously been.

By 18 November 1941, the British 8th Army under Auchinleck had pushed Rommel back from Sidi Barani past Benghazi to Marsa el Brega in a straight fight. But with Malta temporarily silenced, Rommel was able to push 'The Desert Rats' back all the way past Auchinleck's starting line to a tiny unknown village called El Alamein, which he reached at the start of July 1942, just as Malta began to make her presence felt again. His supply convoys were losing more and more ships now that the tiny Mediterranean island was reactivated and, consequently, the Afrika Korps was in bad shape to resist Montgomery's hard push westwards which he launched at the end of October 1942.

Stalingrad – the turning point

Far reaching events were, meanwhile, taking place on the Russian front. The whole of the X and part of the XI German Army Corps had been surrounded by Soviet troops in the Demyansk region after a vigorous and confident offensive by four Russian armies acting in concert. For some 100,000 German soldiers, trapped as the enemy's pincers closed around them, their only hope lay in an airlift by the Luftwaffe to fly in desperately needed provisions. But could it be done? Troops within the pocket speedily cleared two landing grounds for the Junkers Ju 52s, the first of which landed on 20 February 1942, full to the brim with food and miscellaneous equipment. Messerschmitt Bf 109s of J.G. 3 and 51 flew escort missions when they could to ward off waiting Russian LaG and MiG fighters. Despite temperatures of some forty degrees below zero, a miracle was achieved and the ground troops received adequate supplies to keep them intact as a fighting force from mid-February to mid-May, after which they succeeded in fighting their way through to freedom. A second, much smaller airlift was organized when some 3,500 men of an infantry division were cut off by the Russians at Kholm. The supplies, dropped in canisters this time, sustained the troops until another infantry division fought through to free them.

Although these airlifts were successful in themselves, they had the disastrous effect of making Hitler believe the Luftwaffe's transport force could feed and equip any number of stranded ground troops, no matter how large. This was very far from the truth, as events during the winter of 1942–3 at Stalingrad were soon to illustrate all too vividly.

For the Luftwaffe, as for the Wehrmacht, the Battle of Stalingrad was a nightmare of totally unprecedented proportions. The VI Army under General Friedrich Paulus had fought a long, hard campaign to capture almost all of the city when, on 19 November 1942, the Russians launched their counter-attack with such ferocity and in such strength that the Germans found themselves totally cut off a mere five days later. Some quarter of a million men were then trapped in and around the city – far too large a number for the Third Reich to afford to lose. Nor did the Soviet offensive stop on the Don, but swept some 50–75 miles further westwards, coming to a halt on the River Chir. In an equally swift and deadly fashion came another enemy for the Germans – 'General Winter'.

Paulus hedged his bets. He wanted to hold on where he was and continue fighting, unless any proposed airlift proved inadequate to supply his troops in sufficient quantities, in which case he opted for a break-out. But Hitler uncompromisingly forbad any attempt to breach the encircling Soviet troops. The VI Army, he stated, would stay put! Although no record exists to confirm the assumption that Goering promised his leader that the Luftwaffe could take on the job of furnishing supplies, such undoubtedly happened. When the notion of an airlift became known to Luftwaffe and Wehrmacht leaders, they opposed it *en masse* as completely unworkable. Not only had the weather closed in with a vengeance, but the Luftwaffe's transport fleet simply lacked the numerical strength to supply the stranded men with the 300 tons of material they needed each day to keep going. It was madness.

Madness or not, the Fuehrer insisted it had to be done. But here the weather stepped in. When warm air from Iceland met the bitterly cold air over Stalingrad, they combined to produce dense

fog, zero temperatures, snow storms and sleet. Rubber tyres froze and then cracked, fuel and oil froze, engines froze, and mechanics forced to work in the open and frequently under blizzard conditions suffered in large numbers from frostbite on their hands and faces. Replacing any ordinary engine component at once became a major operation. Although some 320 transport aircraft (the majority of them Junkers Ju 52s) had been assembled, only some 100 could fly at any one time. The Ju 52s lost at Crete and during the Battle of Demyansk could have been employed very usefully at Stalingard, but they were now lost for ever. Consequently, the length and breadth of Germany had to be combed for transport aircraft, and many of those that could be scratched together lacked even basic equipment as radios and guns.

Disaster

The troops at Stalingrad waited impatiently for the airlift to begin, and on 25 November it did. Not, however, with the 300 tons needed, nor with anything like that figure. On the first two days of the lift, the Luftwaffe could manage a paltry 75 tons only. And when heavy blizzards grounded the Ju 52s on the third day, it became clear that the tri-motor transports were not going to succeed unless they received substantial aid. There was no alternative but to use bombers as transports and so, once the decision had been taken, a force of 190 Heinkel He 111s was made available. To shield the overall fleet, fighter *Geschwader* J.G. 3 'Udet' was also flung in. And to make Russian tanks think twice about any further offensives on the ground, two *Gruppen* of Stukas and anti-tank aircraft were also scraped together.

With the Heinkels and Junkers flying more or less continuously, the tonnage delivered gradually crept up until it reached 100 tons on 30 November. Then more blizzards arrived and, once again, strangled further attempts. On 2 December, the blizzards were followed by ice that froze every engine solid, obliging mechanics to spend many precious hours trying to unfreeze them. Paulus impressed on the Luftwaffe the heart-rending state his men were in and his pleas for greater aid spurred mechanics and aircrews alike to superhuman efforts. From 19 to 21 December, 700 tons were flown in to the beleagured troops and, for a short while, morale lifted slightly. But the inevitable happened, and in rolled the fog again to cripple further flights.

The transport 'fleet', if such a collection of motley, battered aircraft merited such a term, had been operating from two airfields, Tazinskaya and

Morosowskaya, some 50 miles behind the front line. But in late December the Russians stormed over the River Chir towards the airfields that were so vital in trying to meet the VI Army's needs. In a mad, last-minute bid to escape from Tazinskaya as Soviet tank shells burst on the airfield's perimeter, the panicking Ju 52 crews took off at all angles in a state of complete disorder. Shortly afterwards the first Soviet tanks approached Morosowskaya, expecting to enjoy similar success. They were all set to take the airfield when a brief burst of clear weather gave the Stukas of St.G. 2 and twin-engined bombers of K.G. 27, 55 and 100 just the opportunity they required. The Russians were bombed without mercy and their attack, for the time being, petered out. Once the bad weather returned, however, so did the Red Army, and this time it was the Luftwaffe who had to depart in haste. With the loss of these two airfields, the awful fate of the VI Army took a further step nearer realization.

The Luftwaffe was now forced to fly from airfields even further away from Stalingrad but, bad as that blow was, it was not a fraction as important as the loss on 16 January 1943 of the airfield of Pitomnik, situated actually inside the trapped pocket of 250,000 Wehrmacht troops. There remained only one other; the airfield of

Gumrak, a small wreck-strewn strip isolated in a sea of blinding snow. The Luftwaffe strained itself to the limits to find sufficient machines to keep the airlift going, even stealing maritime Kondor aircraft from their bases in France, but nothing they could do would now save the VI Army and everybody knew it. On the night of 21–22 January 1943, the Russians overran Gumrak and the final collapse loomed clear.

On 2 February 1943 the VI Army radioed out one last message in which it said it had fought to the last man. Starved, frostbitten, many wounded and even more without weapons, the 90,000 or so who remained finally capitulated. Their agony was increased by an epidemic of typhus that swept through their ranks carrying off 50,000. All in all, only some 5,000 survived the war to return to their Fatherland: five thousand out of more than a quarter of a million.

That was what the Battle of Stalingrad meant to the Wehrmacht. What did it cost the Luftwaffe? From the end of November 1942 to the end of January 1943, the German air arm lost a total of 490 aircraft, including 266 Ju 52s and 165 He 111s. The lives of hundreds of aircrew were also lost, mainly because of the weather but also because of Soviet fighters and flak.

The Luftwaffe was never to be the same again.

Defending the Reich by Night

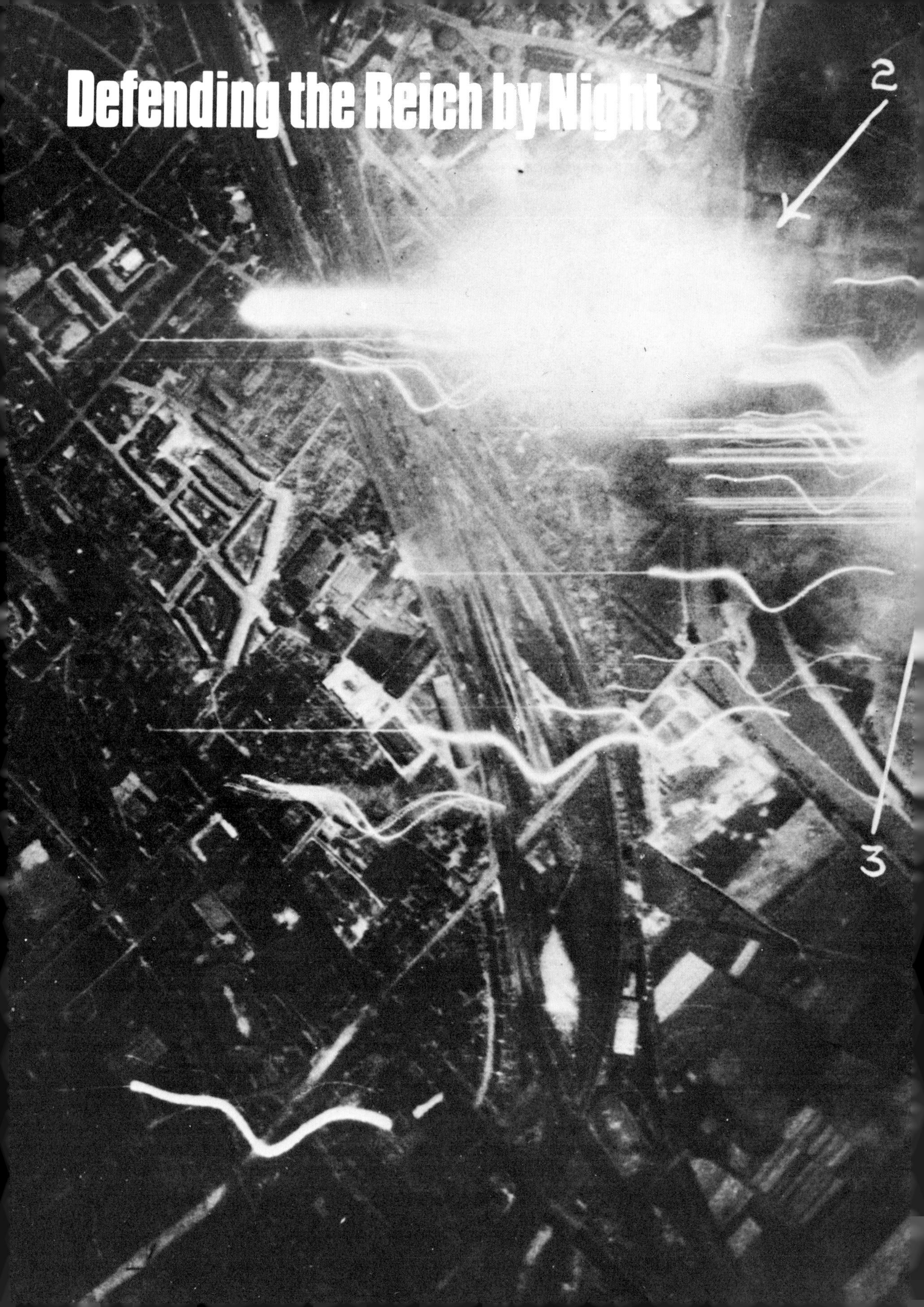

Three thousand, one hundred and eighty aero engines coughed into life on a host of night-shrouded airfields throughout southern England. Sleeping villages and towns shook to the roar of 795 Halifax and Lancaster four-engined bombers flying overhead as another massive armada swung east and headed for an apparently quiet Europe. The night was the 30–31 March 1944; the target was Nuremberg.

German ground radar scanning the Channel soon detected the coming onslaught and already-alerted nightfighter pilots duly took off. The Luftwaffe nightfighter crews were directed to the bomber stream by ground radar stations until they were so close they could switch on their own Lichtenstein S.N.-2 airborne radar sets which they carried in their own aircraft. An R.A.F. Bomber Command Lancaster showed up as a blob of light on a cathode ray tube. The S.N.-2 sets told their operators the bearing, distance and altitude of the intruders, all of which was passed to the pilot until visual contact was made.

The British bomber stream attracted Luftwaffe nightfighters like moths to a candle on this particular night, and some twenty *Gruppen* of the defenders poured in from every direction: the Netherlands, Belgium, northern France and Germany. Once the Messerschmitt Bf 110s and Junkers Ju 88s had penetrated the bomber stream and mixed with it, the rest was far easier for them. The Messerschmitts were equipped with a device known as 'schräge Musik', which consisted of two cannon so mounted as to emerge facing semi-vertical from the roof of the cockpit. In addition to this ingenious invention on the Bf 110, both types were equipped with formidable batteries of cannon and machine guns in their noses.

Although the British doggedly held their course and fought back bravely, their losses mounted. First ten, then twenty, then thirty of the large Halifaxes and Lancasters blazed like torches in the brightly moonlit night.

When it was all over and the tattered remnants had returned, it was found that the Luftwaffe had claimed a grand total of ninety-five of their number destroyed in the air, while a further twelve were so badly damaged they were written off on landing. A further fifty-nine sustained serious damage. In other words, twelve per cent of the attacking force had been lost. It was too much, far too much, and it shook Bomber Command to its very foundations.

Although 30–31 March 1944 represented the Luftwaffe's greatest single success in the skies at night, it was by no means the only occasion German nightfighters shot down large numbers of Bomber Command aircraft. On 17 April 1943, for example, Bomber Command lost thirty-six bombers out of 327 attacking Pilsen in Czechoslovakia, and on 29 May a further thirty-three out of 719 attacking Wuppertal-Barmen. Fifty-six of the big British bombers were lost on 23 August when a total of 727 attacked Berlin, and shortly afterwards, during a further attack on the capital, German nightfighters shot down forty-seven.

But the story behind these and other successes began some years before, in 1940 in fact, when the Luftwaffe established its very first *Gruppe* of nightfighters to combat the small-scale raids then being mounted by R.A.F. twin-engined bombers, such as Wellingtons and Whitleys. There was no ground nor airborne radar to aid the nightfighter crews in those days, however, and pilots had to rely on the keenness of their own eyesight. Although sufficient successes were chalked up to gain the nightfighter arm recognition, it soon became apparent that some more sophisticated system for catching the Reich's uninvited visitors was needed.

Nightfighter arm established

On 16 October 1940, Josef Kammhuber was promoted to Major-General and made 'General of Night Fighters'. Kammhuber, a born organizer, rapidly identified what the two roles of the nightfighter arm should be: firstly, defensive; secondly, offensive. To fulfil the first role he strung belts of searchlights across the paths usually taken by the British bombers so they could be illuminated as they flew over. In the summer of the following year he added a chain of ground radar stations, each of which was allocated a codename, such as 'Polar bear', 'Tiger', 'Lion', 'Jaguar' or 'Dolphin'. Equipped with Wuerzburg radar sets that indicated the direction, range and altitude of incoming aircraft, the stations were built along the Danish, Dutch and Belgian coastlines. Now the nightfighters could be directed to their prey by ground radar controllers. Liaising with flak regiments, Kammhuber also established joint nightfighter-flak zones of defence.

To fulfil the second role, that of offensive operations, Kammhuber created a long-range nightfighter *Gruppe* and sent it on intruder operations over airfields known to be used by Bomber Command. German radio experts tuned their sets in to those used by R.A.F. bombers and, consequently, knew precisely which British airfields were preparing for a raid that night. It was then simply a question of catching them on the ground or in mid-take-off. If the raiders had just returned from an attack over Europe, then the heavily-armed Dornier Do 17s and Junkers Ju 88s joined their landing circle and destroyed their victims in that fashion. Attacks were made much more effective if fragmentation bombs were showered on the bombers while they were still taxi-ing prior to take-off.

Unfortunately for the nightfighter arm, Hitler then decreed that the offensive intruder operations were to cease forthwith. He based his decision on psychological considerations; the morale of the German people was lifted only if they could actually see the enemy being destroyed or witness his battered remains on Reich territory. The logic of the Fuehrer's argument was no doubt faulty, but Kammhuber was nonetheless obliged to call the operations to an abrupt halt. This admirable man was struck another blow by the German leader when Hitler removed the searchlights from his command and handed them over to the regional *Gauleiters*.

Undeterred, Kammhuber pressed on. A significant stride forward was taken on 9 August 1941 when airborne radar in the form of Lichtenstein B/C was carried for the first time by an aircraft, a Bf 110, in flight. This meant that once within striking distance of the bomber stream the airborne radar operator could take

over from the ground controller and guide the pilot himself. The airborne radar was more precise in its target indication over the last few thousand yards than ground radar and thus helped tighten the effectiveness of the system as a whole. Kammhuber, meanwhile, added more and more ground stations to his organisation and housed the larger divisional operations rooms in bomb-proof shelters. The only snag in the overall picture was that each station could direct only one airborne fighter at a time. This was fine as long as Bomber Command sent their aircraft over in long drifting streams stretching over many miles, but if they decided to change to tighter, more compact formations that would pass through the radar belt in a far shorter time, Kammhuber's defence might not be able to cope.

In early 1942 three important events in Great Britain all occurred within a short time of each other. Four-engined Halifax, Stirling and Lancaster bombers began to reach squadrons in significant numbers; British scientists developed a new navigational system called 'Gee', which enabled its operator to pinpoint the bomber's precise position; and Air Marshal Sir Arthur 'Bomber' Harris was appointed as Bomber Command's new chief. One of the first decisions Harris took was to send his aircraft over in tight formations.

The new C.-in-C. believed that the morale of the German civilian population could be fatally weakened if their cities were pulverized, large numbers of people rendered homeless, communications heavily disrupted, and general chaos created. A new directive was issued which stipulated that 'the morale of the enemy civilian population and, in particular, of the industrial workers' should be the first object of bombing operations, while it was emphasized by the Chief of Air Staff, Sir Charles Portal, that it was the cities' built-up areas that should be the crews' main aiming-points. Harris later wrote: 'The aiming-points were usually right in the centre of the town'.

Thus the scene was set for the series of giant nocturnal clashes over German-occupied Europe and Germany itself.

In three consecutive months of 1942 – March, April and May – Harris struck. These first three rounds undoubtedly went to the R.A.F. as Luebeck, Rostock and Cologne were gutted by intense fires caused by the inclusion of a great number of incendiaries among the high-explosive bombs. In the Luebeck raid, over 500 people were killed and double that number of houses smashed. Only eight of the bombers were downed by defending fighters. Three-fifths of the old city of Rostock was burned out when R.A.F. bombers hit it on four consecutive nights during April, but worse was to follow in May when Harris launched his first-ever 1,000 bomber raid, with Cologne the selected target. Harris made the people of Cologne suffer as no German civilians had been forced to suffer before. Although the Luftwaffe hacked down thirty-six of his four-engined strategic bombers, he flattened 600 acres of the city in one fell swoop, making hundreds homeless and causing untold agony. By June, however, the *Nachtjagdgeschwader* (Nightfighter Units) had recovered from their shock and succeeded in destroying almost fifty of the nocturnal raiders flying against Bremen.

Window

In the latter half of 1942, the British introduced a trio of new devices intended to hamper the Luftwaffe's chances of making successful interceptions, and to improve the accuracy of their own bombing. First employed operationally in August 1942, Moonshine radio countermeasures equipment was designed to confuse German early-warning radar. In December of the same year a new navigation and bombing aid named 'Oboe' was used, and in January 1943 British bombers began carrying H.2 S. sets, which gave their operators a radar picture of the territory over which the bombers were flying. August 1942 saw the creation of the famous Pathfinders, whose job it was to locate and illuminate targets with brightly coloured flares on which the main following force would concentrate their bombing.

With his bombing theories sanctioned by the Casablanca Conference held in January 1943, Harris was ready in March of that year to open

the so-called Battle of the Ruhr. The Battle lasted four months, during which he struck not only at targets within the Ruhr industrial region, but at cities all over Germany. The Luftwaffe took a steady but unspectacular toll of the attackers and succeeded in shooting down a total of 872 of them during the four-month period. Yet this figure represented only one-twentieth of the bombers despatched and encouraged Harris to devise even greater blows.

On 24 July 1943 his greatest blow so far fell, and with devasting effectiveness. To their intense consternation Luftwaffe radar operators found the screens of their Freya and Wuerzburg sets presenting them with indecipherable dancing muddles of light spots, among which those representing the British bombers could not be distinguished. They were blinded! The nightfighters waited in vain for instructions from the ground controllers, who could not give the headings they required. The whole nightfighter arm had been neutralized within seconds! The fighters flew round in circles, occasionally darting here and there, but without definite information on the whereabouts of the British force they had no alternative but to land again.

The R.A.F. bombers in the air that night had released hundreds of thousands of strips of silver paper code-named 'Window'. Cut to half the wavelength used by the Wuerzburg sets, they simply threw the German radar impulses back as they drifted down to earth in enormous clouds. This had the effect of producing myriad echoes on the Wuerzburgs' screens which coalesced to form a band of continuous and impenetrable light.

Thus protected, the raiders flew on undisturbed towards their target, Hamburg. 'Operation Gomorrah' was the unpleasant name given by the Allies to the planned erasion of this ancient Hanseatic city. The overall attack was divided into a number of separate blows. On the night of 24–25 July 1943, almost 800 R.A.F. bombers hit the city, after which 235 U.S.A.A.F. Flying Fortresses struck it twice more on the twenty-fifth and twenty-sixth. On the night of 27 July, 722 R.A.F. aircraft offloaded their bombs over the crippled blazing city, after which a further 699 struck yet again on the night of the twenty-ninth. A further attack on the night of 2 August was only half-successful, owing to heavy cloud over the target area. Even though blinded by 'Window', Luftwaffe fighter crews could not stand helplessly by and watch the destruction of thousands of their own people. Single- and twin-engined aircraft flocked to the scene and, aided by the terrific glare below them, sent 87 of the bombers down to the funeral pyre they had created themselves.

Wilde Sau

For Hamburg, the attack spelled terror on an unimaginable scale. More than a quarter of a million homes were destroyed, about 180 factories blown to pieces, almost 200,000 tons of shipping sunk in the port, and some eight square miles of the city laid waste. It was only in 1957 that the Hamburg authorities were able to estimate the total number of dead: some 50,000, including about 7,000 infants and young people. Hundreds of fires had joined to produce a phenomenon called a firestorm. The air above the centre of a firestorm is heated to such extreme temperatures (up to 1,000°C) that a violent upsurge of air occurs which, in turn, pulls fresh air from around the perimeters of the storm into its centre. The force with which the surrounding air is swept in is so great that trees and houses can be dragged into the storm with it. People and vehicles are flicked like dust particles into the heart of the furnace. The firestorm experienced by Hamburg assumed a life of its own and leapt across the city, consuming everything in its path. What did not burn, melted.

And yet, at the very moment it appeared the R.A.F. had dealt the Luftwaffe's nightfighter arm a killing stroke, the *Nachtjagdgeschwader* bounced back into being as an efficient, if somewhat desperate, force still to be reckoned with. This lightning recovery was thanks to Major Hajo Herrmann, who pioneered a new nightfighting technique aptly dubbed *Wilde Sau* (Wild Boars). It did not call for the nightfighters to try to intercept the British, which they could not have done without radar anyway, but to race straight to the anticipated target and maintain patrol there

until the first bombers were illuminated by searchlights. The fighters would then pounce, taking maximum advantage of the fact that their quarry was silhouetted against the fires created below. The obvious disadvantage of the system was that the *Wilde Sau* pilots might go charging off across the night sky to patrol over a certain town while, in reality, the British formations were heading for another town. To try to negate this disadvantage, Herrmann had his single-seat fighters equipped with extra 400-litre tanks, which gave them a far greater range. Goering ordered Herrmann to establish his own *Geschwader*, J.G. 300, but after a while a further order came through to the effect that all nightfighter units were to adopt this new, unorthodox method of fighting. It was a measure born of desperation, but, much to everybody's surprise, it worked better than anticipated.

On the night of 17–18 August 1943, *Wilde Sau* pilots collected over Berlin, convinced that their capital was the R.A.F.'s target of the night. It was not. Peenemuende was, and suffered accordingly. Six nights later, however, they got it right. This time Berlin was the correct target. With many of the 727 attacking four-engined bombers held by the huge city's searchlights and many more silhouetted against the fires below, the defenders threw themselves into battle with gusto, shooting down a healthy total of fifty-six. When Harris sent his bombers back to Berlin a week later, Herrmann and his men shot down a further forty-seven.

However, *Wilde Sau* tactics were costing the

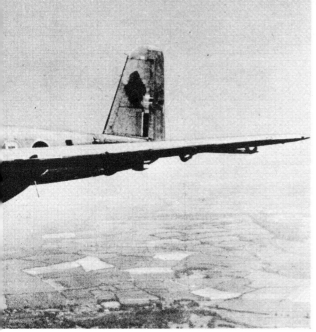

Luftwaffe a good deal of aircraft, too. Single-engined aircraft did not make good nightfighters, and losses were heavy. Herrmann had been using day fighters by night as well, and it soon became obvious that the aircraft would not stand up to the strain of 'round the clock' combat. An increasing number of them became unserviceable, and combined with the fact that pilots frequently guessed the bombers' targets incorrectly, the *Wilde Sau* technique disintegrated. But even as the Wild Boars faded away, German scientists perfected a new airborne radar for twin-engined fighters; one that could not be effected by 'Window'.

Back in possession of effective radar, nightfighter crews soon started to inflict telling losses on the British again. A mere six months after Hamburg, the R.A.F. had to face the distasteful fact that it had not won command of the air, nor anything like it.

When, on the night of 19–20 February 1944, Harris sent 823 strategic bombers off against Leipzig, nightfighter units made a perfect interception and harried their foes to and from the target. The following morning the burnt-out carcasses of seventy-eight of them littered a path across Europe. On 24–25 March, the following month, the Luftwaffe Messerschmitts and Junkers accounted for a further seventy-two from a force intent on raiding Berlin. The climax came, as recounted at the opening of this chapter, on the night of 30–31 March 1944 when the *Nachtjagdgeschwader* shot down ninety-five bombers attacking Nuremberg.

Ambitious plans for the expansion of the nightfighter arm had, meanwhile, been formulated by Kammhuber. He sent them in the form of a memorandum to Hitler, and when he was ordered some while later to present himself to the Fuehrer, he automatically assumed they would discuss his proposals in greater detail. Such was not the case. The German leader had completely lost his temper over some statistics relating to American aircraft production that Kammhuber had included in his document. Hitler described them as 'nonsense' and stated dogmatically that they were grossly inflated. The architect of Germany's nightfighter force had to stand by like a schoolboy while Hitler gave him a good dressing down. Kammhuber was then summarily dismissed from the Fuehrer's presence in disgrace and was later removed from his post, sent, perhaps banished would be more appropriate, to Norway. The fortunes of the arm poor Kammhuber created had waxed and waned throughout the war, but in the latter half of 1944 they started on an increasingly downward trend from which they would never recover.

The first of a series of paralysing blows fell in June 1944 when the Allies invaded Europe. Once the Anglo-Commonwealth-American forces had fought their way out of Normandy, they speedily set about capturing the coastal radar stations on which the nightfighter crews depended for their directions to incoming bomber formations. As station after station went off the air, so the warning times that nightfighter units were accustomed to receiving were drastically cut.

The following month Allied scientists were presented with a brand new and completely intact Junkers 88G-1 after its pilot had become disorientated and landed at Woodbridge in Essex, under the impression he was touching down at his home base. The Ju 88 was equipped with the very latest German search and detection equipment, comprising SN-2, Flensburg and Naxos. Working flat out, the scientists, just ten days later, presented Bomber Command with a new type of 'Window' which would, once again, 'blind' Luftwaffe radar operators. To the nightfighter crews' intense frustration, their SN-2 sets soon began displaying the same meaningless jumbles of light that the first type of 'Window' had so successfully produced about a year earlier. Deprived of their coastal stations and carrying radar sets that told them nothing, the number of 'kills' they registered plummeted.

The most crippling blow of all, however, resulted from the Americans' 'oil offensive'. U.S.A.A.F. daylight bombers had been concentrating their attacks on synthetic oil plants and storage points, with the result that German fuel reserves dwindled away to a fraction of their former volume in late-1944. The nightfighter arm was badly affected and defensive operations had to be cut to the minimum. Right in the middle of this chaotic situation, dismayed crews then received the order that they were to mount nocturnal ground-attack missions in a desperate bid to slow up the Allied rate of advance. Nightfighting is one thing, but low-level flying at night is quite another, and one that requires a specialized technique of its own. The pilots had not received training for it and casualties rapidly escalated.

It was supremely ironic that German aircraft production was at this juncture leaping ahead, thanks to timely dispersal of facilities and the rapidity with which bombed factories could be repaired again. Starved of fuel, deprived of their ground radar stations and blinded by 'Window', the only thing the nightfighter units could rely on with some confidence in 1944 was that losses would be made good again. On the last day of that year the nightfighter arm could boast a strength of 913 aircraft. Admittedly this figure had fallen to just under 500 by early April 1945 but, had sufficient fuel and effective radar equipment been available, even this number would have inflicted heavy casualties on an enemy.

The R.A.F. was already wresting control of the night skies from the Luftwaffe by greater and greater degrees. Now they sent Mosquito nightfighters over Europe to search out and destroy the Bf 110s and Ju 88s. The Mosquito possessed a superb performance far in excess of its two principle adversaries, although it was matched by the very few Heinkel He 219 Uhu nightfighters in service. The He 219 was one of the Luftwaffe's great 'lost opportunities' (see section on this aircraft), and had it been introduced into really large-scale service early in the war, the German air force might have been able to inflict unacceptably high losses on Bomber Command right from the start. For example, fourteen British bombers and six Mosquitoes were shot down by I/N.J.G. 1. in their first half-dozen sorties while flying examples of this remarkable warplane.

Dresden

Maimed as the nightfighter units were by the events outlined above, they were consequently in no position to repel further R.A.F. raids. So when, on the night of 13 February 1945, the R.A.F. and U.S.A.A.F. combined to turn the city of Dresden into a barbaric scene of unspeakable mass destruction, the nightfighters had to sit impotently by. German refugees fleeing the advancing Soviet army had flooded the city a short while before the attack, and this factor alone guaranteed high civilian casualties. In the event more than 100,000 people died as a firestorm of massive proportions swept the city, devouring everything in its path. Some 650,000 incendiaries were specially included to encourage Dresden to burn, and burn it certainly did! Many accounts of the night when Dresden died have been written, some subjective, some objective, and it is outside the scope of this book to discuss the morality of this or any other raid carried out by the R.A.F. Nevertheless, readers might care to ask themselves in exactly what way an attack delivered only some three months before the war's end, which killed more people than either of the Americans' nuclear attacks on Japan, and which killed in one burst more people than died in Luftwaffe attacks on Great Britain throughout the whole of the Second World War, contributed towards hastening the conclusion of hostilities. For the purposes of this short study, the ease with which the Allies wreaked such devastation does amply illustrate the depths of ineffectiveness to which the Luftwaffe's nightfighter force had sunk.

130

Fighting the Americans

Not a single **German** bomb dropped on the American city of Washington in the Second World War, nor on New York, nor Boston, nor Los Angeles. The Old World of Europe never attempted, nor even gave much consideration to attempting, to enter the skies of the New. The citizens of the United States had, perhaps, always taken this for granted. Europe was a remote place both geographically and, to many people, emotionally.

Perhaps it was because no American woman nor child died under the impact of Luftwaffe bombs that the American air force – the U.S.A.A.F. – could afford to view the European air war with a certain clinical detachment. They adhered to the theory that daylight precision bombing of industrial targets by massed formations of well-armed aircraft would do far more than night bombing of civilian cities to bring the war to a rapid end and, unencumbered by the emotional reactions of the British to the Blitz and Coventry, they were determined to prove their theories correct when the first elements of the American 8th Air Force landed in England on 12 May 1942.

The Royal Air Force was not slow to warn its new allies that German fighter defences would inflict heavy losses on unescorted daylight formations. After all, was that not the reason the R.A.F. itself had been obliged to mount its raids under cover of night? The newcomers listened, but remained unconvinced.

The U.S.A.A.F. operated two main types of four-engined bomber, the Boeing B-17 Flying Fortress and the Consolidated B-24 Liberator. Although greater numbers of Liberators were built than any other type of American aircraft, they saw widespread service throughout the world and, consequently, the multi-engined type most clearly identified with the American daylight offensive over Europe itself is the Flying Fortress.

As it was with the Fortress that the Americans intended to battle their way through defending German fighters to their targets and, hopefully, back again, it is worth having a look at the bomber on which so much hope was pinned.

There is no denying that the B-17 was a fine machine. The B-17E, with which the first U.S. squadrons in England were equipped, was fitted out with a formidable array of thirteen 0.3 in.

and 0.5 in. calibre machine-guns, each of which featured a good sight accurate to more than half a mile. With a crew of ten, the 'E' was powered by four 1,200 h.p. engines that gave it a maximum speed of 318 m.p.h., and carrying a maximum of 2,490 gallons of fuel it had a range of 3,300 miles. A wide variety of ordnance loads could be delivered, comprising, for example, twenty 100lb bombs, eight 500lb bombs or two 2,000lb bombs. The 'F', a progressive development, incorporated more than 400 changes, including new engines and propellers, a new ball-turret and additional machine-guns in the nose, greater fuel capacity, and a more efficient bomb-aiming system. A further development, the 'G', saw the introduction of a 'chin' gun turret as standard equipment, which gave this model a total defensive armament of thirteen 0.5 in. machine-guns effectively located in chin, nose, dorsal, central fuselage, ventral, waist and tail positions. The maximum bomb load that this mark could carry on very short-range missions was a spectacular 17,600lb.

When fully loaded, however, neither the 'E' nor the 'F' could manage much more than 180 m.p.h., which gave the Luftwaffe's Bf 109s and Fw 190s a handsome speed advantage. Neither could the large U.S. bombers attain the same altitudes as the German fighters. Their main hope lay, as they were well aware, in concentrating their massive fire-power into a semi-impenetrable defensive shield against which the tiny attacking fighters would batter themselves in vain. Certainly, any single fighter 'caught' in their joint fire would be instantly destroyed. A further weakness of the first B-17s, and one the Luftwaffe soon discovered, lay in the disposition of their protective armour-plating for crew members. Although there were more than twenty such pieces of plating, not a single one had been designed to protect the unfortunate crew from frontal attacks.

Successes against U.S.A.A.F.

A new chapter in the air war was opened with the first American attack on Germany, launched by the 8th Air Force on 19 January 1943 against Wilhelmshaven. Encouraged by the lack of opposition, the B-17s returned to the same target towards the end of the same month. This time the Luftwaffe did react, but with great caution. It was as if two boxers were circling each other, neither certain of his opponent's hitting power. Isolated attacks were made by Focke Wulf Fw 190s of J.G. 1, which shot down three B-17s – by no means a great feat of arms. The American fliers became more confident of their tactics while the R.A.F. watched with interest. If only the Americans had known it, though, one small flaw already manifested itself in that the B-17s' gunners had claimed twenty-two Luftwaffe fighters destroyed during the two Wilhelmshaven attacks whereas, in fact, only seven were lost. It was natural enough; if ten or twenty U.S. gunners all fired furiously away at the same single German fighter and it spun down pouring smoke, then all ten or twenty gunners would claim it destroyed. Each man would swear in the best of faith that it was he who had 'destroyed' a Bf 109 or Fw 190. The degree by which the B-17 gunners' claims exceeded their actual score of kills became more and more ludicrous as the war went on. At one point, they claimed they had shot down so many defending German fighters that, if their claims had born any realistic relationship to the actual number destroyed, the Luftwaffe force in the west would have promptly ceased to exist.

The following month, February, saw the Luftwaffe gradually throw off its initial caution and experiment to find the best means of attacking these impressive giants. Now the B-17s' frontal weakness was discovered, and Luftwaffe *Jagdgeschwader* adapted their tactics accordingly. No longer did the tiny German fighters approach the Fortresses from the beam or rear; now they rushed in with all guns firing at the front of the American formations. It required a lot of nerve to fly a fighter right through a mass of bombers all travelling in the opposite direction, but more and more German pilots realized it was the only way of making any impression on the hosts of American aircraft now flying over their Fatherland. Sure enough, the Germans had found the Americans' Achilles' heel and losses began mounting. A total of twenty-two 'Forts' was shot down during February.

Determinedly, the bomber aircrews persisted in their task and mounted raids of greater strength. On 17 April 1943, 115 Flying Fortresses flew out to hit the Focke Wulf assembly plant situated at Bremen. The Luftwaffe reacted with fury and succeeded in sending down sixteen B-17s and damaging a further forty-four. In mid-June, sixty Fortresses raided military targets at Kiel but lost a further twenty-two of their number. No less than 170 B-17s were damaged and 16 destroyed by defending German fighters when 363 attacked synthetic rubber plants at Huls later in June. By the time 'blitz week' loomed up at the end of that month, there were plenty of ominous signs for 8th Air Force crews to contemplate. The Americans mounted six raids during the week itself and caused a considerable amount of devastation, but only at a perilously high cost. Eighty-eight Fortresses and their crews were lost and it immediately became apparent that the Luftwaffe was successfully taking the measure of their new enemy's attacks.

Nor did it appear that the Americans' precision raids against industrial targets were having any effect on German aircraft production. Fighter production was, in fact, proceeding in leaps and bounds. Although the Russian front gulped down Luftwaffe aircraft and aircrews in vast numbers, and relatively few of the fighters produced were therefore available to be committed to the defence of Germany, nevertheless the figure of 500 fighters produced each month in autumn 1942 grew to 700 in March 1943, more than 800 the following month, and almost 1,000 in June.

The U.S.A.A.F.'s faith in daylight precision bombing had, however, been confirmed in a directive issued after the historic Casablanca Conference held in January 1943. The directive, in fact, sanctioned both the R.A.F.'s and the U.S.A.A.F.'s widely differing methods of bombing Germany and occupied-Europe. 'Bomber' Harris seized on a portion of the directive which said that '. . . the undermining of the morale of the German people to a point where their capacity for armed resistance is fatally weakened' should be achieved by bombing as justification for his belief in mass R.A.F. night attacks.

Brigadier-General Ira C. Eaker, 8th Air Force chief, had his faith in pinpoint daylight attacks confirmed when the directive issued a list of priority military targets that had to be destroyed by bombing. At the top were submarine and aircraft construction industries. The directive also mentioned 'the progressive destruction and dislocation of the German military, industrial and economic system', which undoubtedly reinforced Eaker's beliefs. Just as Harris left the conference secure in the knowledge that his method had been blessed, so Eaker left secure in the knowledge that his had been given an equal blessing. The net result was that Germany's cities were bombed by Harris by night and her industries by Eaker by day. The 'round-the-clock' bombing of the Third Reich was becoming fact as the conference broke up.

American losses mount

The Luftwaffe was inflicting such heavy losses on Fortress formations over the Continent that Eaker had urgently to consider how they could be reduced. The obvious answer lay in an escort fighter that could shepherd the vulnerable bombers all the way to even the most distant target and back. But no such fighter existed. The R.A.F. Spitfire could manage a puny penetration of only some 175 miles, which allowed it to reach Amsterdam and back. That was obviously no good to a man who wanted to fly into Germany itself. An improvement came in June 1943 when American P-47 Thunderbolt fighters escorted the B-17 bombers to a penetration of some 230 miles, which just about reached Luxembourg. After that, however, they had to turn back for lack of fuel, thus leaving the Fortresses unprotected for the rest of their flight. By equipping the Thunderbolts with belly fuel tanks, the Americans gave them a penetration of some 375 miles in August, which allowed them to escort the bombers to targets within the Ruhr industrial region of Germany. Yet vital targets still lay outside this area, and as the U.S.A.A.F. did not find the answer to its problems for some months after that, the Fortress formations had to fly without long-range fighter cover throughout 1943.

The Luftwaffe frequently took advantage of this fact. On 1 August, for example, defending German fighters shot down 54 B-24 Liberators out of a total of 175 attacking the Ploesti oil refineries in Romania. Heavy flak over the target disrupted the B-24 formations, after which fighters of I/J.G. 4, IV/J.G. 27 and IV/N.J.G. 6 harried the unfortunate Americans without let-up. Seven of the four-engined bombers had to land in neutral Turkey and a further three crashed in the sea. As for the refineries, although they were badly hit, production was soon back to normal.

In the face of such losses the 8th Air Force might have been expected to loose confidence in daylight attacks. But they did not. In fact, they pushed energetically ahead with further plans, including one that called for a 'double-blow' against two military targets deep inside Germany and well outside the range of the escorting fighters.

17 August 1943

The two targets were aircraft production factories at Regensburg and ball-bearing factories at Schweinfurt. Much ingenuity went into the planning of this particular attack and it was hoped that German fighter and ball-bearing production would be seriously set back as a result. The plan called for the 4th Bombardment Wing of the 8th Air Force, equipped with B-17s, to hit Regensburg and then turn south-south-east over Italy, cross the Mediterranean and land at Allied airfields in north Africa. Fortresses of the 1st Bombardment Wing would follow more or less directly on their heels, bomb Schweinfurt, turn around, and fly back to England. It was hoped that German fighters, having attacked the Fortresses of the 4th Wing, would be back at their bases rearming and refuelling when the bombers of the 1st Wing passed overhead shortly afterwards. Timing was a critically important factor.

In the event, the plan was thrown out of key by bad weather over England, and although the Regensburg force got under way on time, the Schweinfurt force was held back. This meant, of course, that the German fighters would have time to land and take off again.

On 17 August 1943 the big bombers lifted off

from their bases in southern England and headed towards Regensburg. They were escorted by P-47s until the Belgian-German border was reached, whereupon the fighters had to turn back. With the departure of the escort, all hell was let loose as Luftwaffe fighters poured in to the attack from every direction. Single-engined Bf 109s and Fw 190s attacked with machine guns and cannon from the sides as well as from the front as they usually did. Twin-engined Bf 110s loosed off underwing rockets into the compact formations from outside the range of the Americans' guns, and Junkers Ju 88 nightfighters actually dropped fragmentation bombs on the Fortresses from above. Some B-17s disappeared from view in sudden and spectacular explosions, others shed wings and tails before hurtling earthwards, while yet more simply disintegrated. The sky was a mass of burning fuel tanks and swaying parachutes. With their turn southwards towards Italy, however, the U.S. force succeeded in surprising the Luftwaffe pilots to such an extent that only very minimal opposition was pitted against them. The Germans had obviously expected the Americans to return to Britain.

Unaware of the fate experienced by their colleagues, the second task force bound for Schweinfurt approached Europe under strong fighter protection. This time the Luftwaffe did not wait for the escort to run low on fuel and turn back before it attacked. Fw 190s and Bf 109s tangled with Spitfires over the Netherlands but did not succeed in penetrating the bombers' defensive fighter screen. Before long the Spitfires and Thunderbolts had to leave the B-17s on their own to battle the lengthy distance to the target, and when they turned around the Fortresses were assailed by German fighters from all sides. Some 300 Luftwaffe fighters of J.G. 1, 2, 3, 11, 25, 26, 50 and 300 and elements of J.G. 27 and 54 and Z.G. 26 took to the air that day in defence of their homeland, and started the business of exacting a heavy toll in relays. As one unit disengaged and flew away to refuel and return, so another or others took its place. Bf 109s and Bf 110s launched rockets into the American formations and machine-gun and cannon attacks

were pressed home at close range. A whole variety of enemy types attacked the bombers, including twin-engined Fw 189s, Me 210s, and Do 217s, and the U.S. fliers noted that the German aircraft were being controlled by a twin-engined type flying outside the range of their guns. Not only were the attacks made from in front but from both sides simultaneously and from below. After the Fortresses had dropped their bombs and turned around to head back to England, they were subjected to further attacks that continued even after they had picked up their escort of Thunderbolts over north-eastern Belgium.

After the bombers had landed, the count began. It was found that a devastating total of sixty of the bombers attacking both targets had been lost. This picture was further blackened when the units that had landed in Africa flew home. They had left a further sixty aircraft, beyond repair, in Africa and had lost a further three over the Mediterranean.

The bombers' gunners had claimed an astronomical 228 German fighters destroyed in both missions. The real number was twenty-five.

After all that, had Schweinfurt been erased from the map? Far from it! Some of the plant sustained medium damage, some very light, and some had not even been touched. With typical Teutonic rapidity and thoroughness, repairs started right away and all the raid really did was interrupt production for approximately a month.

That was 17 August 1943.

'Black Thursday'

The Americans' answer was, as always, to press on. During September, replacement units arrived in England with new aircraft, including the model 'G' Flying Fortress equipped with ball and chain turrets, the latter to counter the Luftwaffe's frontal attacks. However, German fighter units, now concentrated in Germany itself, continued to better their attackers whenever the opposing sides met. Simple statistics tell the story: on 6 September, 45 out of 388 bombers were lost; on 9 October a further 28 were lost; and on 10 October another 30. In fact, between 8 and 14 October, the Americans lost almost 150 bombers. To gauge how many aircrew were killed, wounded or taken prisoner, simply add a nought to the number of bombers lost, for every bomber carried ten crew members.

Owing to the speed with which ball-bearing

production had been restored to normal at Schweinfurt, another raid on the plant was scheduled for 14 October. The 1st and 3rd Bombardment Divisions of the 8th Air Force carried out this attack and, once again, the Americans suffered appalling casualties at the hands of the defending fighters. Out of the 260 aircraft that bombed, 65 were lost, 12 more damaged beyond repair, and a further 121 damaged to a lesser extent. The U.S. public was fed the usual stories about the targets being all but wiped out and the terrific numbers of German aircraft shot down, but this did not prevent the *Washington Post* from carrying the headline '60 Forts Lost'. Subsequently, 14 October was nicknamed 'Black Thursday' by the U.S.A.A.F.

Semi-total loss of production of ball-bearings at Schweinfurt lasted for some six weeks only. A mere 80 of the 1,100 or so H.E. bombs dropped landed fair and square on the factory complex, yet more than 600 8th Air Force personnel were lost. After the second raid on Schweinfurt the Americans had to face the fact that they had lost one in three of their U.K.-based bombers. No air force can stand that type of attrition for long. The R.A.F. advised their allies to do what they had done themselves – turn to nocturnal bombing – but the Americans refused to do this. In any case, R.A.F. fliers were being subjected to some pretty heavy losses themselves in the night skies over Europe during that phase of the war.

The Mustang

No, the answer was not to switch to night bombing, but to develop and produce a fighter aircraft with a first-class performance and a range that would take it all the way to the bombers' targets and back again. And this is precisely what the Americans did.

The result was the North American P-51 Mustang. To this aircraft must go the distinction of establishing, more than any other single type of Allied aircraft, air supremacy over Europe during daylight hours. Sleek, speedy and well armed, the Mustang possessed an enormous range – enough for it to be flown all the way to Berlin and back. From 1 December 1943, when the Mustang made its combat début with the 8th Air Force, the effectiveness of the German fighter force was destined to decline and finally fade away almost altogether. It was probably the finest fighter produced by the Allies and must rank as one the four truly immortal fighters to emerge from the Second World War, along with the Spitfire, the Messerschmitt Bf 109 and the Mitsubishi Zero-Sen.

A necessary prerequisite to the Normandy landing was the destruction of the Luftwaffe. It was fully realized by the Allies that if the Luftwaffe were to establish aerial supremacy over the landing beaches, then the result could well be a debacle. So 'Operation Argument' was launched in early 1944 to destroy the German fighter-producing factories. Its deadline for completion was 1 March that year.

Unfortunately for the Americans, when they launched the plan's first attack on 11 January 1944, an insufficient number of Mustangs had arrived in England to provide the bombers with a fully effective defensive screen. Only forty-nine of the new P-51s were available, and these could hardly be expected to ward off the Luftwaffe fighters on their own after the other escort types had been obliged to return to their home bases. Although the top echelons of the Luftwaffe were dismayed to find that their enemy had produced a fighter with seemingly miraculous powers of flight endurance, on this occasion the German fighters penetrated the Mustangs' screen and assaulted the bombers with their customary ferocity. A total of sixty of the four-engined bombers were lost, plus five fighters. The bombers' gunners claimed 152 Luftwaffe fighters destroyed, but in fact the real number was 39.

Five weeks later, when the U.S.A.A.F. launched its second attack of the operation against Germany's aircraft factories, the situation was radically different. A formidable force of fighters, including American Lightnings and Thunderbolts, American and British Mustangs and British Spitfires, had been assembled to cover the bombers. Almost 950 bombers, shielded by this armada of some 700 fighters, set out to pulverize the Third Reich's combat aircraft production plants. The Bf 109 and Fw 190 pilots threw themselves against the massed formations of attackers but, try as they did, could not penetrate the defensive screen. The battle rapidly degenerated into a mass of individual fighter-versus-fighter dogfights through which the main bomber stream passed almost unscathed. The heavy losses of some fifty to sixty machines that the U.S.A.A.F. had been experiencing on some attacks fell, on this occasion, to a much more acceptable twenty-one. The fighters in general, and the Mustang in particular, were doing the trick.

The Allies did not ease the pressure. That night the British sent off some 600 bombers against aircraft production facilities in the Stuttgart region, and no sooner had they landed than the Americans launched further attacks. Encouraged by the ineffectiveness of the Luftwaffe's aerial opposition and the good bombing results so far obtained, the U.S.A.A.F. launched a further two raids the following day, 22 February 1944. But this time they came unstuck and, once again, the *Jagdgeschwader* proved they were still capable of inflicting heavy losses when American fighters were absent. The plan called for a double blow by both the 8th Air Force operating from England and the 15th Air Force flying from bases captured in Italy. However, bad weather over England prevented two-thirds of the 8th's attacking force from forming into formations properly, thus necessitating their recall, and fighters of J.G. 1 and 11 neatly converged on the remaining third before it was scheduled to pick up its Mustang escort. With the Mustangs not yet on the scene and the bombers protected only by a handful of Thunderbolts, the German fighters wreaked havoc on the bombers, shooting down forty-one of them. The 15th Air Force coming up from Italy ran into trouble too, although on a smaller scale, and lost fourteen of their aircraft to German attacks.

Two days later, on 24 February, the Americans returned, this time with 600 bombers. Against the 15th Air Force flying up from Italy, the Luftwaffe sent up Bf 109s and rocket-firing Bf 110s, which shot down a full twenty per cent of the attacking force – seventeen out of a total of eighty-seven

bombers. A larger number of 8th Air Force bombers was meanwhile flying deep into Reich territory from bases in England. They got through the German defensive screen and hit Schweinfurt (again) so hard that it was still burning furiously the following night, when 700 Lancasters of R.A.F. Bomber Command struck the target once more.

'Operation Argument' came to a spectacular climax on 25 February with another in the series of joint attacks from Italy and England. The Luftwaffe fared well against the force of 176 unescorted bombers coming up from the south and shot down a healthy total of 33. But the force flying in from England was escorted by Mustangs, and the German fighters quickly found themselves entangled with their nimble opponents. Not often able to penetrate the Mustangs' shield, they managed to destroy only 31 of the 738 bombers taking part. The Messerschmitt factories were smashed to smithereens by the Americans' accurate bombing during the attack but, just to make quite certain, the R.A.F. returned to the same target that night.

Dwindling effectiveness

As the weeks rolled by, and the Americans showed themselves over Europe in greater and greater strength, it became apparent that their long-range fighter aircraft were not only effectively shielding the bomber formations but that they were also succeeding in shooting down the intercepting German fighters in increasing numbers. With the Russian, Italian and Channel fronts swallowing so many aircraft, the Luftwaffe could ill afford to lose many on the home defence front. Nor could it afford to lose the growing number of pilots sacrificing their lives in daily combat with the American fighter aircraft now appearing over every part of Germany. As more and more of the older, experienced aces succumbed to the Americans' numerical superiority, so their places were taken by youngsters whose training had sometimes been sketchy to say the least. It has been said that the Reich lost as many as 1,000 pilots between January and April 1944. This illustrates how

successfully the long-range Mustangs were
keeping down American losses while sending the
Germans' sky high.

It is ironic that one of the Luftwaffe's most
successful battles should also have sounded the
death knell for their fighter arm. It took place
on 6 March 1944, when a couple of hundred
Luftwaffe fighters scrambled to meet large
U.S.A.A.F. formations heading for Berlin. A
running battle developed, stretching over
hundreds of miles, during which the gallant
German fighter pilots ran the gauntlet time and
again to get through the escorting American
fighters and hit the bombers. They did so in
brilliant fashion and sent an excellent sixty-nine
of them down. They also shot down eleven U.S.
fighters. More than neutralizing their spectacular
success, however, was the crushing fact that they
lost no fewer than eighty of their own fighters
that day. An air force the size of the Luftwaffe,
forced to do combat on so many fronts
simultaneously, simply could not stand losses of
that magnitude.

Just two days later, on 8 March, and again
on 22 March, the U.S.A.A.F. launched further
massive attacks. A considerably reduced number
of Luftwaffe interceptors did battle on the first
occasion and were lucky to shoot down 37 of
the almost 600 bombers involved. Only a very
light defensive screen of Luftwaffe fighters took
off to meet the incoming American force on the
second occasion and, becoming entangled with the
bombers' escort on contact, failed to destroy a
single one.

Although 'Operation Argument' failed to
dislocate the Reich's aircraft production plants,
this now ceased to matter as the P-47s and P-51s
were doing an excellent job of destroying
Germany's aircraft in the air. In the first five
months of 1944, so fateful from the Luftwaffe's
point of view, the Americans stole control of the
skies from their enemy and hung grimly on to it.

Totally outnumbered

For the Luftwaffe there was a further change
for the worse when the American escort fighters
were given permission to range freely over and
around the bomber formations and even leave
them if an extra kill were scored. So it was that
the role of the escorting fighters changed from
defensive to offensive. No longer did they adhere
strictly to that area of sky occupied by the
unwieldy four-engined bombers, but gave chase
over miles and miles of countryside whenever the
Bf 109s and Fw 190s put in an appearance.
German losses continued to grow until, in May
1944, the Luftwaffe possessed less than 250
single-engined and 40 twin-engined fighters with
which to protect the whole of the Fatherland in
the west. Since the strength of the U.S.A.A.F.
fighter escorts frequently doubled or even trebled
that figure, the futility of the Germans' position
is obvious. Indeed, the twin-engined Bf 110s could
no longer afford to do battle with the faster, more
manoeuvrable Mustangs in daylight. When
forty-three of them intercepted an 8th Air Force
bomber stream on 16 March 1944, twenty-six were
shot down and the remainder hounded all the
way back to their home bases by the exultant
Americans. The place for the Bf 110 was in the
night sky – not the day!

An attempt to break through the vicious circle
now enclosing them was made by the Luftwaffe's
fighter pilots when they formed 'light' and 'heavy'
interceptor units to undertake different roles. The
'light' fighters would ward off the Mustangs while
the 'heavy' fighters, well-armoured and
heavily-armed, would attempt to hit the bombers.
It was a measure born of desperation and did
not work. The Mustangs, with their superior
numbers, penetrated the 'light' units' defensive
screen and slaughtered the 'heavy' fighters, which
suffered a performance penalty because of the
amount of weighty armour they carried.

Outnumbered in the air, with many of their
aces killed, matched by aircraft either their equal
or superior in performance, the Luftwaffe's fighter
pilots could clearly see the outcome of this
unequal struggle, although they continued to fight
with spirit until the end. They were further badly
hampered by another factor, and one of supreme
importance. The Americans had now switched the
focus of their attacks to the Reich's oil industry,
and with crippling success.

Götterdämmerung : The Twilight of the Gods

So seriously did the American offensive against Germany's oil producing industry limit her ability to wage war that it is only remarkable, from the viewpoint of a modern reader, that the offensive was not undertaken much earlier than May 1944.

Oil and fuel were as vital to the needs of the Reich's mechanized fighting forces as food and water were to the soldiers themselves. It did not matter how successful Germany was in producing fighter aircraft and thwarting 'Operation Argument' if there was no fuel for the new aircraft once they rolled off the production line.

After the German failure to bring down 'the whole rotten edifice' of the Soviet Union in one lightning campaign in 1941, further extensive and fuel-consuming campaigns had to be fought in 1942. The U.S.S.R.'s enemies had not reckoned with this, and, consequently, found themselves severely short of fuel in September of that year. Thanks to some drastic conservation measures, Germany managed to keep fighting, but she recognized anew just how vital to her needs it was to keep stocks of fuel at high level. The man appointed to overhaul the country's whole production of synthetic fuel was Albert Speer. He

did a good job, ensuring not only that current production was retained but that it rapidly headed upwards.

In late 1943, stocks stood at 400,000 tons, this figure rising to over half a million tons by April 1944. But when, in May 1944, the Americans switched their bombing attacks to oil production plants, Germany was in for a hard time. Bearing in mind that at this stage of the aerial war the Luftwaffe's fighter arm in the west was experiencing heavy losses and that comparatively few American bombers were, therefore, being shot down, it soon became clear that the Reich's vulnerable production plants were going to be well and truly hammered and that there was little the Luftwaffe could do to protect them.

In May, production fell to under 200,000 tons, which was bad enough, but the following month it once again plummeted, this time to just over 50,000 tons. As Allied bombs rained down on plant after plant, production took a further turn for the worse in July, when 35,000 tons were produced, this figure falling to 16,000 tons for August and a ridiculous 7,000 tons for September. As production began drying up, further and further restrictions were placed on the Luftwaffe's flying. The bomber units were the first to feel the pinch, after which training programmes were drastically cut. Curbs on fighter-bomber ground support missions were then made and, finally, fighter operations in the west were affected. As new aircraft left the production lines they received only the barest minimum testing before being delivered to their operational units.

War on two fronts

After the failure of Hitler's 'Operation Zitadelle (Citadel)', designed to restore the initiative to the Wehrmacht after the disaster of Stalingrad by eliminating the Russian salient around the city of Kursk, things went from bad to worse for the Germans along the entire eastern front. The Axis lacked the strength to outnumber its opponents along the whole of the front, and could only manage to gain localized superiority through the concentration of forces at one specific point. This, however, involved denuding portions of the front of men and machines, thus making such areas doubly vulnerable to Soviet attacks. Stalin skilfully switched his offensives against areas in which he knew the Germans were weak, and this policy paid stunning dividends. In July 1943 the Wehrmacht stood some 100 miles from Moscow and about 50 miles from Kursk. A year later the situation had radically changed. In the centre, the army had been driven back some 300 miles from the Soviet capital, and, in the southern central area, some 400 miles from Kursk right into Poland.

The Russians were poised to smash through deep into the heart of German Europe in 1944.

As the war progressed, Goering had increasing cause to regret his inability to strike at the Soviet aircraft plants safe in the Ural mountains. Working day and night without a German soldier within hundreds of miles, the personnel at the aircraft factories turned out bombers, ground attack aircraft, fighters and reconnaissance machines in their hundreds and thousands. While the Allies pounded the Reich's aircraft plants to rubble, their own large-scale production plants in

the U.S.A. and the U.S.S.R. went untouched by the Luftwaffe.

Nor was it simply a question of quantity. The quality of the Soviet aircraft with which the German fighter pilots had to deal daily had also risen substantially. The Russian air force phased out the old biplanes it had been equipped with at the war's start as quickly as possible and re-equipped with monoplane fighters with enclosed cockpits, retractable undercarriages and good cannon/machine-gun armament. In 1942 the most important fighter it possessed was the Lavochkin LaGG-3, which was armed with one cannon and three machine-guns, powered by a 1,100 h.p. engine, and flew at 348 m.p.h. Its successor, the La-5, made its first battle appearance over Stalingrad; its 1,640h.p. engine giving it a speed of just over 400m.p.h. A further design, the La-7, flew at 413m.p.h., was armed with three cannon, six rocket missiles, and could carry over 400lb of bombs. And just before the end of the war, the Soviet air arm took delivery of the Lavochkin La-9, an outstanding fighter in all respects, featuring a speed of 428m.p.h. and a four cannon armament.

The MiG concern also produced some excellent fighter aircraft. Although handicapped by poor powers of manoeuvrability, the MiG-3 could attain the high speed (for late 1941) of 407m.p.h. Small numbers of a later model, the MiG-5, saw service in 1943, while the following year saw the flight testing of the MiG-7 high-altitude interceptor fighter equipped with long-span wings and a pressure cockpit. Some idea of the advanced thinking then current among Soviet aircraft designers may be gauged from the fact that in 1945 Mikoyan had a fighter called the I-250 which was powered by a conventional liquid-cooled piston engine and a ramjet! The I-250 attained a maximum speed of more than 500m.p.h.

Russia's third big design bureau was headed by Alexander Yakovlev. Yakovlev also produced some good fighter designs, including the Yak-9 and the Yak-9U; the latter, armed with a cannon and two machine-guns, could attain 415m.p.h. Reckoned by some pilots to be superior to the Spitfire, the Yak-3 excelled at low altitude combat against Luftwaffe fighters and featured a good rate of climb, a maximum speed of over 400m.p.h. and a mixed cannon/machine-gun armament.

The Allies' choice of Normandy for the invasion caught Nazi Germany off balance. As far as the Luftwaffe was concerned, even if it had known in advance of its enemy's D-Day plans in detail, it is doubtful if it could have contributed substantially to their defeat. For the sad fact was that this once proud force had declined so greatly that it possessed under 200 bombers and little more than 100 fighters in a suitable position to strike at the bridgeheads that the Allies quickly established. The Allies, on the other hand, flung an impregnable umbrella of almost 9,000 fighters and bombers over their vessels and troops to keep the Luftwaffe at bay and smite the Wehrmacht. Two German fighters flew over the D-Day beaches, but two were not enough. Not even 200, nor perhaps 2,000 (had they been available) would have sufficed to pierce the gigantic fleets of U.S.A.A.F. and R.A.F. aircraft flying over France and the Channel.

Staggering as it was under the Allies' numerical superiority, the Luftwaffe was not yet a completely spent force, however. It was still destined to see two major pieces of action, the first of which was a brilliant success. On the night of 21–22 June 1944, more than 100 B-17 Flying Fortresses and their P-51 Mustang escort fighters landed at the Russian airfield of Poltava, having bombed their target and flown over the Reich undisturbed. It was the first of what the Americans termed 'Pendulum attacks'. Most of the few long-range bombers that Germany had been able to produce took off to deliver a surprise blow against the crowded Soviet base. Three whole *Kampfgeschwader* delivered their bomb loads with accuracy right among the parked U.S. aircraft and succeeded in wiping out forty-three of the bombers and fifteen of the fighters. The attack illustrated only too vividly what the Luftwaffe could have done had it possessed a large and efficient long-range bomber force much earlier in the war.

The second action took place on New Year's Day, 1945, and consisted of a series of surprise attacks in strength against airfields used by the

R.A.F. and U.S.A.A.F. in western Europe. Codenamed 'Operation Bodenplatte (Ground Plate)', the attacks envisaged using just about every piston-engined fighter remaining to the Luftwaffe in the west. It was a desperate last fling and, as they retired early to bed the night before, many Luftwaffe pilots hoped their enemy would be too befuddled by New Year celebrations to put up much resistance. Such was not to be the case.

Despite the very thorough briefing they had received, pilots of some units failed to locate their targets while others, who did manage to find them, delivered their attacks in a clumsy amateur fashion. Chaos on some Allied airfields was caused, however, as the German formations swept in from low altitude and machine-gunned Allied aircraft standing in vulnerable positions in the open-air. For example, two Canadian squadrons equipped with Typhoon fighter bombers were caught while taxi-ing and speedily decimated. But after the dust had settled, one thing became clear. The Luftwaffe had lost more aircraft than the Allies as a result of heavy and accurate ack-ack fire and patrolling Allied fighters. Aviation historians have quoted different casualty figures for both sides in the attack, assessing Luftwaffe losses at between 200 and 300 aircraft. But the exact figure did not, in a sense, matter, for whatever it was, it meant that the Luftwaffe's piston-engined units in the west had disappeared in one last glorious but futile burst of energy.

Even then, as the clock of fate stood at almost midnight, the German air force managed to pull a final rabbit out of the top hat. Or, to be more precise, two rabbits. The first was the Messerschmitt Me 262 jet fighter; the second was the Arado Ar 234 jet bomber.

The story of the Me 262 was simultaneously one of the most inspiring and the most hopeless of the Luftwaffe's last minute attempts to beat the Allies' superior numbers by its own superior technology.

The aircraft's superbly streamlined aerodynamic shape alone sufficed to demonstrate how far in advance of all other countries' aircraft designers were those of Germany. With its swept-back wings, tricycle undercarriage and heavy nose armament, and powered by two axial-flow Junkers Jumo turbojets, the Me 262 instantly rendered every Allied piston-engined fighter obsolete overnight. It was capable of 542 m.p.h. at almost 20,000 ft – a stunning speed that enabled it to pierce the Americans' defensive Mustang screens with ease. It is quite reasonable to assume that if Germany had possessed large numbers of this type a good deal earlier in the war, the U.S.A.A.F.'s daylight bombing offensive would have been completely crushed.

What went wrong? Two things. Firstly, Hitler's obsession with bomber aircraft led him to issue one of his infamous 'Fuehrer Orders', to the effect that the Me 262 was to be produced primarily as a *Blitzbomber* and not as a fighter, the role for which this outstanding aircraft had been designed and in which, if allowed, it would have excelled. Secondly, and probably more importantly, Junkers failed to produce large numbers of jet engines for the type until September/October 1944, owing to technical difficulties that took a long time to overcome. When, on 4 November 1944, Hitler finally relented and gave permission for the type to be produced as a fighter, all was set for the mass production of this potentially war-winning machine. But by November 1944 the war was in an extremely advanced stage; in the air, the Allies jointly held absolute sway. The tragedy was that the Me 262 simply appeared too late (and therefore could be manufactured in too few numbers) to affect the outcome of the war itself, or even of the aerial war, to any marked degree.

Although the jet fighter saw service with several units, the two with which it is today most closely associated are *Jagdgeschwader* J.G. 7 and the elite *Jagdverband* 44.

Formed in December 1944 and destined to defend its shrinking homeland until the very end, J.G. 7 was to claim no less than 427 enemy aircraft destroyed, including more than 300 four-engined heavy bombers. Adolf Galland, dismissed by Goering from his position as General of Fighters, collected the most famous and talented of the Luftwaffe's remaining aces together and

established his own jet fighter unit, J.V. 44. Becoming operational only at the very end of March 1945, J.V. 44 nevertheless claimed about 50 kills before the war's end. With Allied aircraft everywhere, the men of J.V. 44 could not always afford to use conventional airfields as these were obviously open to air attack, so they conducted many of their operations from an intact stretch of autobahn running between Munich and Augsburg, taking great pains over the immediate camouflaging and concealment of their machines when not in the air. Their main task was to strike at the omnipresent B-17 Flying Fortress formations, which they attacked in flights of three aircraft at a time. When carrying racks of 24 R4M missiles under the wings of each jet, the pilots of J.V. 44 launched all two dozen simultaneously, watching for the instant destruction of any B-17 that had the misfortune to be in the path of one of these deadly air-to-air weapons. But on 3 May 1945, J.V. 44's airfield of Salzburg-Maxglan was overrun by U.S. tanks.

It is interesting to note that between ten and a dozen examples of a nightfighter model, the Me 262B-1a/U1, were delivered to the Luftwaffe for the nocturnal defence of Berlin. Unfortunately, no details of their operational history have come to light.

The other type of jet that saw action with the Luftwaffe was the Arado Ar 234 bomber. Although far too few entered service to affect the eventual outcome of the ground battles then raging over central Europe, the type did succeed in forcing the Allies to mount large-scale standing patrols to try to intercept the odd one or two that crossed the front line from time to time. This had the effect of tying down substantial numbers of fighter aircraft that could otherwise have undertaken more valuable duties elsewhere.

As in the case of the Me 262, the Ar 234's performance included a speed (474 m.p.h.) that rendered it all but immune from Allied interception, and not many were destroyed. Capable of carrying 3,300lb of bombs externally and flying for a thousand miles at high altitude, the Ar 234 featured an exceptionally streamlined nose area, the whole nose itself comprising transparent curved cockpit panels through which the one-man crew could obtain a magnificent view forwards, upwards, downwards and on both sides. A periscope mounted on the cockpit roof gave him rearward vision.

It is doubtful if more than 100 Ar 234s saw action before the termination of hostilities, the sole bomber unit to be equipped with them being K.G. 76 in October 1944. Based initially at Achmer near Osnabrueck, K.G. 76 flew its jets at low level against the Remagen bridge, captured by the Americans to storm across the Rhine into the heart of Germany. But dogged by bad weather, heavy defensive ack-ack and plenty of American fighters, the unit failed to score direct hits on the bridge. The pilots of K.G. 76 continued, however, to mount attacks against a variety of Allied ground targets, not only from their base at Osnabrueck but also from airfields in Luebeck and Schleswig, to which they were later obliged to evacuate owing to the rapid rate at which Germany was shrinking.

Because flying at low level severely reduced the aircraft's radius of action, various experiments were undertaken to give it a greater range. One of the most interesting involved stripping a V1 flying bomb of its pulse jet and fin, filling it with jet fuel, and towing it behind an Ar 234 by means of a rigid tow. Although this idea was actually tried out in practice, it was never used operationally. When the war ended, dozens of these advanced jet bombers stood around Luftwaffe airfields in various states of damage waiting for the Allies to grab them, effect repairs and test them themselves.

No account of the Luftwaffe's aircraft and operations would be complete without mention of the fantastic Messerschmitt Me 163 Komet. Literally a glider with a liquid rocket motor installed in it, this tiny aeroplane was capable of attaining the then unheard of speed of 596m.p.h., albeit for only a few minutes. Only one unit was equipped with this last-ditch fighter, J.G.400, formed in March-May 1944 and first seeing action in August of that year. Komets of this unit were flown against American bomber formations and made an incredible sight as they zoomed at terrific speed through the ponderous masses of four-engined B-17s. After reaching sufficient altitude, an Me 163 pilot had only two and a half minutes' rocket power remaining before his motor consumed all the fuel and ceased functioning, whereupon the aircraft became a highly vulnerable 'glider'. Although the men and machines of II/K.G. 400 fought until the end of the war, it is very doubtful if they and their fiery steeds accounted for more than a dozen Allied aircraft in combat.

Collapse

And so the dark shadows of defeat hemmed Germany in. She was caught in a massive vice between overwhelmingly powerful enemies in both west and east and finally crushed between them. The fates of millions of men and women were caught up and blown about like chaff in the wind as the Third Reich entered its last agonizing death throes and finally succumbed.

What of the Luftwaffe? It stood in sad disarray with most of its remaining aircraft empty of fuel, damaged in combat, or deliberately disabled to prevent their further use. Some of the more advanced jet types were eagerly seized by the British, Americans, Russians and French, spirited away and then repaired and tested in flight. They learned a lot from the technical information gained in these tests.

A large variety of projects was in hand when Germany collapsed, most of them employing the very latest in aeronautical technology and relying on jet power for great speed. They included such designs as the Junkers EF 130 flying wing bomber, powered by four jets and supposedly capable of 625m.p.h.: the Focke Wulf 1000 × 1000 × 1000 bomber designed to carry 1,000 kilograms of bombs (2,200lb) at 1,000 kilometres an hour (625m.p.h.) for 1,000 kilometres (625 miles): the revolutionary Focke Wulf Triebfluegel vertical take-off and landing jet fighter that featured a helicopter-like set of 'rotor blades', at the tips of which were installed dumpy jet pods: and the Gotha P60C nightfighter that carried its two jet engines in tandem, mounted above and below the rear of the fuselage.